SPRINGER SERIES
IN PERCEPTION ENGINEERING

Series Editor: Ramesh C. Jain

Springer Series
In Perception Engineering

Thomas M. Strat

Natural Object Recognition

With 48 illustrations

Springer-Verlag

New York Berlin Heidelberg London Paris
Tokyo Hong Kong Barcelona Budapest

Thomas M. Strat
Artificial Intelligence Center
SRI International
Room EK- 266
333 Ravenswood Avenue
Menlo Park, CA 94025 USA

Series Editor
Ramesh C. Jain
Electrical Engineering and
    Computer Science Department
University of Michigan
Ann Arbor, MI 48109 USA

Library of Congress Cataloging-in-Publication Data
Strat, Thomas M.
        Natural object recognition / Thomas M. Strat.
            p. cm. -- (Springer series in perception engineering)
        Includes bibliographical references.
        ISBN 0-387-97832-1
        1. Optical pattern recognition. 2. Computer vision. I. Title.
    II. Series.
    TA1632.S82 1992
        006.3'7--dc20   92-1511

Printed on acid-free paper.

Production managed by Karen Phillips; manufacturing supervised by Robert Paella.
Photocomposed pages prepared from the author's L^AT_EX file.
Printed and bound by Edwards Brothers, Inc., Ann Arbor, MI.
Printed in the United States of America.

9 8 7 6 5 4 3 2 1

ISBN 0-387-97832-1 Springer-Verlag New York Berlin Heidelberg
ISBN 3-540-97832-1 Springer-Verlag Berlin Heidelberg New York

PREFACE

The title is intentionally ambiguous. The research reported here has led to the development of a new paradigm for visual recognition of *natural objects*. It is my hope that this novel design may someday also be regarded as a natural approach to *object recognition*.

Thomas M. Strat

April 9, 1992

ABSTRACT

An autonomous vehicle that is to operate outdoors must be able to recognize features of the natural world as they appear in ground-level imagery. Geometric reconstruction alone is insufficient for an agent to plan its actions intelligently — objects in the world must be recognized, and not just located.

Most work in visual recognition by computer has focused on recognizing objects by their geometric shape, or by the presence or absence of some prespecified collection of locally measurable attributes (e.g., spectral reflectance, texture, or distinguished markings). On the other hand, most entities in the natural world defy compact description of their shapes, and have no characteristic features that are sufficient for discrimination among classes. (For example, what features of a rock could be used to distinguish rocks from other naturally occurring objects?) As a result, image-understanding research has achieved little success towards recognition in natural scenes.

This book offers a new approach to visual recognition that avoids these limitations and has been used to recognize trees, bushes, grass, and trails in ground-level scenes of a natural environment. Reliable recognition is achieved by employing an architecture with a number of innovative aspects. These include: context-controlled generation of hypotheses instead of universal partitioning; a hypothesis comparison scheme that allows a linear growth in computational complexity as the recognition vocabulary is increased; recognition at the level of complete contexts instead of individual objects; and provisions for stored knowledge to guide processing at all levels.

Recognition results are added to a persistent, labeled, three-dimensional model of the environment which is used as context for interpreting subsequent imagery. In this way, the system constructs a description of the objects it sees, and, at the same time, improves its recognition abilities by exploiting the context provided by what it has previously recognized.

ACKNOWLEDGMENTS

This work would not have been possible without the stimulating environment and abundant resources provided by the Perception Group of SRI's Artificial Intelligence Center. The Condor system makes use of code provided by many members of this group:

- Steve Barnard — Cyclops dense stereo depth maps (on Connection Machine)

- Pascal Fua — Software for striations and snake operators

- Marsha Jo Hannah — STEREOSYS binocular stereo compilation

- Ken Laws — KNIFE segmentation system

- Yvan Leclerc — POLYSEG segmentation system (on Connection Machine)

- John Lowrance — Grasper II (coauthor)

- Lynn Quam — ImagCalc and the Cartographic Modeling Environment

- Grahame Smith — Core Knowledge Structure (coauthor)

- Helen Wolf — Linear delineation and region growing algorithms

I am indebted to all of the above plus Harlyn Baker, Aaron Bobick, Tom Garvey, Mike Genesereth, Andy Hanson, Jean-Claude Latombe, Sandy Pentland, and Marty Tenenbaum, for sharing their insight into the problems addressed here and into the field of computer vision in general. Marty Fischler, through his keen insight into the field of computer vision, has motivated, inspired, and influenced nearly every aspect of this work.

CONTENTS

LIST OF FIGURES

LIST OF TABLES

1

INTRODUCTION

1.1 Motivation

Much early machine-vision research in the modern signals-to-symbols paradigm was concerned with the interpretation of scenes from the "blocks world." Line drawings of simple geometric objects were analyzed to infer the shapes of individual objects. More recent research has focused on the recognition of man-made objects, such as industrial parts in a factory setting, roads in an aerial photograph, and furniture in an office environment. In these systems, several complicating factors that were not present in the blocks world had to be addressed: namely noisy images, imperfect geometric models, and complex lighting. The complexity of description necessary for recognition was greater than that required for the blocks world. A logical next step in this progression is the interpretation of ground-level images of natural outdoor scenes. In the manufactured world, three-dimensional (3D) edges and surfaces are an adequate intermediate representation, but for the natural world, such shape descriptions are insufficient and perhaps inappropriate. By designing a vision system for interpreting ground-level scenes of the outdoor world, we hope to provide a new basis for a theory of computational image understanding in complex domains.

Many computer vision systems have been devised to recover the three-dimensional location and orientation of surfaces from image data. However, shape recovery is only a part of the functionality that is required of a vision system for autonomous robots that are to operate outdoors. Outdoor robots are of practical importance in roles such as industrial robots for construction site preparation and waste management, military systems for reconnaissance and target acquisition, and agricultural systems for crop planting and harvesting. In order for these systems to interact intelligently with their environments, they must be able to recognize things in terms of physical attributes and semantic qualities, not just shapes. While geometric reconstruction is often sufficient to infer the identity of a man-made artifact, it is insufficient for the recognition of many natural objects. To illustrate this point, consider a robot observing the scene in Figure 1.1. To plan a path across the scene, the robot needs to understand that a river is in the way, it must reason that the current is too swift for it to wade across, and it must estimate the physical properties of the bank and of the rocks and logs that might be used as stepping stones. Perceptual recognition capabilities that are sufficient to enable such reasoning have been developed only for some very specific tasks in constrained domains such as inspection of welds and identification of machined parts on an assembly line. The understanding of scenes from a complex domain such as the natural outdoor world is not possible at present.

Any autonomous system must have a means for perceiving its environment. Many computational vision systems produce image-like, iconic descriptions of a scene. In contrast, formal reasoning and planning systems rely on stylized, symbolic representations. For example, the robot considering the scene in Figure 1.1 might reason that if no bridge exists, it could go upstream until it found a suitable crossing site. However, evaluating the "bridge-exists" predicate requires an understanding that is far beyond the current capability of computational vision. This mismatch between the perceptual demands of symbolic reasoning and the iconic capabilities of machine vision has been dubbed the "pixels to predicates problem," and is a fundamental obstacle to the construction of intelligent autonomous systems [Pentland 1986b]. The research reported here is an attempt to bridge this gap in the domain of natural outdoor scenes.

1.2   Issues

A common paradigm for machine vision research has been to choose a structured domain in which some capability could be achieved and then attempt to extrapolate those results to less constrained (i.e. more complex) domains. One of the clearest lessons from research in image understanding has been that systems developed for a particular domain do not generalize to more complex domains. Thus, it is unlikely that we will ever find a solution to the recognition of natural objects such as rivers, trees, or rocks by studying the recognition of machine parts in a bin, or doorframes in a hallway.

FIGURE 1.1. A natural outdoor scene.

We discard the common practice of working in a well-behaved domain where successful recognition is likely, and instead choose to study a complex domain: ground-level imagery of the natural outdoor world. In so doing we hope to gain insight into the deeper problems inherent in visual recognition — problems whose solution might lead to truly flexible, general-purpose machine vision systems.

We have chosen to design an architecture for machine vision that is intended to recognize natural features of the outdoor world. Aside from the practical benefit of developing a system that would enable an autonomous vehicle to navigate in an unmodified outdoor environment, this goal invites research into a number of fundamental issues that are less relevant in simpler domains:

- Computer vision presents the following (chicken and egg) paradox: in order to recognize an object, its surroundings must often be recognized first, but to recognize the surroundings, the object must be recognized first. Is it really necessary to recognize everything at once, or can some things be recognized in isolation? If so, what are they and how can they be recognized? What is a suitable vocabulary for recognition in the natural world?

- Most man-made artifacts can be recognized by the shape of features extracted from an image, but many natural objects cannot. Furthermore, most natural objects have no compact shape description. What representation of shape is useful for describing natural scenes? What role does geometry play in recognizing natural objects? Given that segmentation of natural outdoor imagery is problematic, how should a natural scene be partitioned into discrete components?

- For any object in a given setting, some features in the scene are useful for recognizing the object and others are seemingly irrelevant. What contextual information is sufficient to recognize natural objects? How can these contexts be represented? How can contextual information be used in recognition?

- From a computational standpoint, general-purpose recognition is very hard. Many algorithms that have been proposed are exponential even in simple domains. How can the combinatorics inherent in the recognition problem be contained? What can be done to control the computational complexity of natural object recognition?

- One of the characteristic features of biological vision systems is their ability to learn from experience. A rat in a maze learns a path to a reward, a human learns to recognize a familiar street corner, but computer vision systems forget what they have computed as soon as they are restarted. A perceptual entity should learn from its experience. How can this be accomplished? How can a vision system be designed so that it can make use of newly acquired information?

These issues are fundamental problems that prevent automatic recognition of natural objects, but are less critical in simpler domains. The investigation of these issues in the context of the natural outdoor domain has been the focus of the research presented here. In designing and constructing a complete system for natural object recognition, we have developed solutions to a number of these problems and tested the resulting theories with outdoor imagery.

1.3 Contribution

The judicious use of contextual information has proven to be the key to successful recognition of natural features. The value of context has long been recognized [Garvey 1975], but its use was irrelevant in vision systems devised for recognition in many simpler domains. Our solutions to these issues have been incorporated in a system called Condor (for CONtext-Driven Object Recognition) to demonstrate their validity.

The Condor architecture for using contextual information revolves around four key ideas:

- Use *multiple operators* for extracting features of interest. Individually, each operator may be unreliable, but at least one of them will usually extract the desired feature in any given image. These operators produce hypotheses to be considered for integration into a complete scene description. This process of intelligent hypothesis generation eliminates universal partitioning as a critical first step in recognition.

- Use *mutual consistency* as the basis for determining whether a labeling hypothesis is valid. If a hypothesis is incorrect, it is unlikely to be consistent with a set of other hypotheses that explain the entire image. Recognition at the level of complete contexts rather than individual objects affords a basis for reliable interpretation.

- Test strong hypotheses for consistency before considering weaker ones in order to manage the computational complexity. Hypotheses are ranked by *pairwise comparison* based on the scores of context-dependent evaluation functions. This mechanism identifies the best interpretations early in the search for mutually consistent sets of hypotheses and restricts the computational complexity to growing only linearly with the number of classes to be recognized.

- Use *context* to guide all phases of the computation. Many operators and tests are reliable only in specific contexts; they can be employed sensibly by explicitly modeling and recognizing contexts. A specialized construct known as the context set provides a mechanism for efficiently encoding and invoking contextual knowledge.

These observations form the core of the Condor architecture and are responsible for any success that it has achieved.

A new knowledge representation structure, the *context set*, is introduced and used in Condor. A context set specifies the set of conditions that must hold for an operation to be invoked. We use context sets as the unified representation for the three types of knowledge employed by the system: (i) contexts in which an operator is used to generate candidate hypotheses; (ii) contexts in which two candidates can be compared; and (iii) contexts in which candidates can be considered mutually consistent.

The set of labels for which context sets are provided constitutes the vocabulary for recognition. Unlike previous approaches, this one differentiates between the target vocabulary and the recognition vocabulary. The *target vocabulary*, the set of labels that one is ultimately interested in recognizing from imagery, depends on the intended task. The *recognition vocabulary* contains the target vocabulary plus those additional terms that may be of use in recognizing instances of the target vocabulary. The issue of what terms should be included in the recognition vocabulary is resolved through experimentation with the system. None of the classes of objects in the target vocabulary could be recognized in isolation. However, instances of all classes in the recognition vocabulary have been recognized without knowledge of classes outside that set. For example, Condor has recognized trees without knowing about rivers, but was unable to recognize sky reliably without knowing about such things as a horizon, ground, and foliage.

Many vision systems attempt to analyze images in isolation. Some others are designed to exploit closely spaced image sequences. Condor employs a fully three-dimensional database as its world model and uses it to relate information extracted from sequential images. The results of an interpretation are stored in the world model; they are then available to provide context for analysis of subsequent images. In this way, Condor builds up its expertise over time. A robot exploring a piece of terrain must move slowly at first as it examines everything in fine detail. As the world model is developed, Condor can use more efficient processes in contexts that have become understood to be more highly constrained, and can use special-purpose procedures that become applicable only in those contexts. This gives the robot the ability to learn about its environment and to learn how to recognize something the next time it is seen. Even processing the same image over and over (perhaps while the robot is "sleeping") may permit new information to be extracted and stored, and a better interpretation to be obtained.

1.4 Example of results

Condor has analyzed more than fifty images acquired from a two-square-mile undeveloped portion of the Stanford University campus. These ground-level images represent a cross section of the variability exhibited in this area; they span a two-year period including all seasons and all times of day and feature trees and bushes at all scales.

Input to the recognition system consists of an image (either monochrome, color, or stereo) and, optionally, a database containing map data and previous recognition results. Emphasis has been placed on achieving labeling accuracy while recovering qualitatively correct geometry, rather than reconstructing the precise scene geometry, a topic which has been studied extensively by others. As output, Condor is expected to provide a 3D model of the viewed area, labeled with terms from the recognition vocabulary.

To accomplish this goal, Condor makes use of a knowledge base in the form of a collection of 156 context sets that prescribe which operations to carry out in various circumstances. Some of these context sets are specifically tailored to the experimentation site, while others are of general utility. This knowledge base has enabled recognition of natural scenes with considerable success and has been used to obtain all the results presented in this volume.

As an example, one of the color images that Condor has analyzed is

FIGURE 1.2. A natural outdoor scene of the experimentation site.

FIGURE 1.3. Result of analyzing Figure 1.2.

FIGURE 1.4. A perspective view of the 3D model produced from the analysis of the image shown in Figure 1.2.

reproduced in Figure 1.2 (in black and white). Context provided to Condor at the time of analysis consisted only of a digital terrain model and the forest boundaries as extracted from a map. Condor used this information to recognize the sky, the ground, the grass, and five trees, as shown in Figure 1.3. The result is a 3D model of the scene, whose objects have been labeled by their semantic categories. This model can be viewed from any perspective, such as shown in Figure 1.4.

Substantial experimentation with Condor has been performed to evaluate key issues concerning its competence and limitations. Our conclusions stemming from these tests are:

- The approach is adequate for recognizing, under a variety of viewing conditions, the trees, bushes, trails, and grass that occur in a limited region.

- A reasonably complete 3D model of a large area can be constructed by combining the results from the analysis of individual images.

- Condor's own recognition results can be used as context to enable it to improve its recognition abilities incrementally through experience.

In conclusion, the Condor architecture appears to be well-suited as the basis for an outdoor robotic vision system because it not only learns a description of the host's environment, but also learns how to use that description to achieve still better recognition of natural objects.

2
NATURAL OBJECT RECOGNITION

2.1 Visual capabilities for autonomous robots

If robots are ever to attain versatile and autonomous behavior, it will be necessary to endow them with perceptual abilities that go far beyond the geometric reconstruction that modern robots perform. There is a tremendous difference between the expectations placed by robot designers on a perception system and the capabilities that the field of machine vision has so far provided.

At first glance, it may seem that an accurate three-dimensional geometric model is all that a robot should need to successfully navigate its environment. Why should an agent have to recognize its surroundings?

Imagine a rabbit hopping around in a field. If it didn't know that the blades of grass were flexible, it would have to conclude that the field is impassable. If it attempted to walk across the flat surface of a pond, it would drown. Similarly, an autonomous vehicle that couldn't discriminate between a bush that could be driven over and a rock that could not would have limited navigational ability. Recognition of physical properties is necessary — for survival of a rabbit, and for viability of a robot.

The need for understanding goes beyond physical properties. The rabbit, upon encountering a large blob, had better be able to discern whether it is a tree stump or a wolf. An autonomous construction robot may be given the knowledge that granite can be made into a strong building foundation and that sandstone cannot. If it is to use its knowledge of construction materials, that robot must be able to distinguish the two types of rock. In general, objects in the world must be identified so that an agent's large store of knowledge can be brought to bear. We refer to the process of identification as *semantic recognition*.

Perhaps the most important call for semantic recognition is in support of planning. No agent can be considered intelligent if it lacks the ability to plan its future actions based on current goals. The rabbit, which must decide where it is going to look for food, would starve if it relied on a purely geometric model of its environment because the lack of semantic information would prevent the rabbit from devising a meaningful plan. Planning is just as important for a robot; automated planning has been an area of intense study since the inception of artificial intelligence. AI planners for outdoor robots make reference to such semantic categories as bridge, road, river, and tree — none of which can be instantiated from a purely geometric model.

Finally, there is the need to fill in gaps where information is missing. A robot cannot be expected to have a complete and up-to-date model; it will be limited to knowledge of areas already explored. To infer the shape and appearance of the back side of a tree requires first that the object be recognized as an instance of a tree, so that the appropriate defaults and global shape can be assigned. Completing the unobserved side of a hill requires even more understanding, such as knowledge of drainage, distribution of trees, limits on surface slope, and the like.

Completions along the dimensions of scale and time are also required. One need not recognize individual leaves to infer that there are leaves on a tree. Similarly, the prediction of the appearance of a tree in winter cannot be made without determining if the object is a deciduous tree.

No matter how extensive and detailed is the representation possessed by an agent, it will never be complete for all purposes. Augmenting a geometric model with an understanding of physical and semantic properties gives the agent the ability to infer the information that it cannot sense directly. However, augmentation can take place only if at least part of the scene has been semantically recognized.

In summary, recognition involves more than geometric reconstruction.

2.2   Related research

Recognition is the crucial element of a vision system that is to understand what it sees. The pixels-to-predicates gap is bridged when symbolic labels are assigned to image features.

2.2.1   RECOGNIZING OBJECTS

The term 'recognition' has been used to describe a variety of machine-vision goals based on different assumptions. The vast majority of research on recognition relies on the use of a known geometric model of the object being recognized [Binford 1982]. Such systems are often cast in an industrial setting where one or a small number of parts are to be located within a scene. Historically, some of the earliest work in 3D model recognition was performed in the early 1970s with the aim of finding polyhedra [Roberts 1965, Shirai and Suwa 1971] and generalized cylinders [Agin 1972, Agin and Binford 1973, Nevatia 1974] in light-stripe range data. Examples of more recently implemented systems that successfully use geometric models are 3DPO [Bolles, Horaud, and Hannah 1983], ORA [Huttenlocher and Ullman 1988], and the curved 3D object-positioning system of Ponce and Kriegman [1989]. The goal of these systems is the location and orientation of the objects of interest.

Some research has been directed toward relaxing the strict assumption of a fully specified geometric model. These techniques employ a parameterized model (as in Acronym [Brooks 1983] and One-Eyed Stereo [Strat and Fischler 1986]) or a generic model (as in [Fua and Hanson 1987] and [Kriegman and Binford 1988]). While much less restrictive in scope, these techniques all rely on shape as the primary attribute for recognition.

A third category of recognition research avoids the use of stored geometric models. Recognition is attempted on the basis of cues other than shape, such as size, location, appearance, purpose, and context. Hawkeye [Barrow *et. al.* 1977], MSYS [Barrow and Tenenbaum 1976], and the present approach, Condor, are examples of the few systems that have been designed without a primary reliance on geometric models.

2.2.2   RECOGNIZING NATURAL SCENES

Nearly all research on recognition has been conducted in a context where a precise geometric model of the desired object is known beforehand, and the major goal has been to find a projection of the model that best matches some part of an image. Precise geometric models have proven to be invaluable in many systems that recognize man-made artifacts   [Bolles, Horaud, and Hannah 1983,   Faugeras and Hebert 1983, Goad 1983, Grimson and Lozano-Perez 1984, Ponce and Kriegman 1989].

For the natural world, however, these models are inadequate. Although it may be possible to construct a 3D model of a tree to some level of precision, the model is not likely to be of much use in recognition. Furthermore, no two trees have the same shape, and even individual trees change their appearance and shape over time. Statistical models of natural objects using fractal functions or particle processes are extensively used in computer graphics to render realistic images of natural scenes, but these models are of only limited use in machine vision.

To relax the requirement for complete and accurate models, [Fischler and Elschlager, 1973] introduced the technique of spring-loaded templates, which represent objects as a combination of local appearances and desired relations among them (the "springs"). An object represented in this way is located in an image by using dynamic programming to minimize local and global evaluation functions simultaneously. Some geometric recognition systems, such as ACRONYM [Brooks 1983], accept parameterized models to describe a class of objects, but these too are overly restrictive to be of much use for recognizing natural features. Research at Schlumberger has made extensive use of elastically deformable, symmetry-seeking models to recover the geometry of some natural objects, such as fruits, vegetables, and the grain pattern in a piece of wood [Terzopoulos, Witkin, and Kass 1987].

The interpretation of natural scenes requires methods that do not assume the existence of *a priori* geometric models. The amount of work toward the goal of semantic understanding of natural outdoor scenes has been relatively small and, surprisingly, almost none has occurred in the last ten years. All of these approaches begin by partitioning the image into regions, which presumably mirrors the natural decomposition of the scene into "objects." The regions are then analyzed in one way or another to determine their interrelationships, to merge them into larger regions, and ultimately, to assign to each region a label that categorizes it semantically. The predominance of this approach is surprising, considering that the notion of an "object" in a natural scene is ill-defined. This basic reliance on an initial universal partitioning is a critical weakness that is avoided in the approach taken by Condor.

Sloan used a production system in which domain knowledge is encoded as rules to use in analyzing regions and assigning labels [Sloan 1977]. The approach was handicapped by the use of a single-pass segmentation: if the initial segmentation contained errors (as it surely would), the interpretation would also be wrong. Furthermore, the knowledge base was limited to two-dimensional relations only, had no notion of scale, and could not make use of prior expectations of objects.

Ohta also used a rule-based approach to assign labels to regions generated by a single-pass segmentation [Ohta 1980]. Labels were assigned to regions by matching each region with predefined models of typical region properties. Ohta made the use of color a central concern but his system exhibited many of the same limitations as that of Sloan.

Yakimovsky and Feldman used Bayesian decision theory to label regions [Yakimovsky and Feldman 1973]. Their implementation allowed intermediate results to guide the segmentation by merging regions when doing so was more likely to result in a correct interpretation. Domain knowledge was encoded as conditional probabilities, and prior expectations were incorporated as prior probabilities. The probabilistic approach has several drawbacks, as the estimation of probabilities is notoriously difficult and the final interpretation can be highly dependent on these estimates. Furthermore, probabilistic updating rules invariably require independence assumptions that are seldom warranted in practice. This early approach was also limited to 2D relations and suffered from the restriction that the interpretation of a region depended only upon adjacent regions.

Rosenfeld, Hummel, and Zucker used iterated parallel operations to allow local information to propagate throughout the image in a search for convergence to a consistent interpretation. Their effort was directed toward exploring the mechanisms and computational properties of such a relaxation approach and did not address the interpretation of natural scenes [Rosenfeld, Hummel, and Zucker 1976].

Tenenbaum and Barrow used a relaxation method on natural scenes [Tenenbaum and Barrow 1976]. This approach established a set of possible labels for each region and used Waltz filtering to act on local constraints in an attempt to find a consistent labeling. Variations on this method performed region-merging to generate a more acceptable segmentation and used geometric models when available. In MSYS [Barrow and Tenenbaum 1976], the technique was extended to reason with uncertain information and inexact rules of inference.

Tenenbaum [1973] and Garvey [1975] recognized that feature extraction cannot be performed bottom-up and developed methods that pose perception as a planning problem in order to focus resources on critical subproblems. A given object is found by first planning a strategy that might identify it using simple features in the context of already known facts about the scene, and then executing the plan. This process exploits distinguishing features that can be recognized easily and can be reliably used for classifying an object. Experimentation was performed in the domain of office scenes.

The Schema system of the VISIONS project at the University of Massachusetts is perhaps the only completely implemented system for interpreting ground-level outdoor scenes [Hanson and Riseman 1978, Draper *et. al.* 1989]. In this approach, interpretation of an image involves low-level filtering and segmentation processes and high-level interpretation processes embedded within a blackboard framework. Schemas are used at the higher abstraction levels to control the invocation of relevant knowledge sources. Empirically derived likelihoods guide the interpretation, which is entirely two-dimensional. Nonetheless, this system performs better than any previous approach to outdoor scene interpretation.

There is a large body of literature on the related topics of interpreting aerial imagery (e.g. [Ballard, Brown, and Feldman 1978] and [Nagao and Matsuyama 1980]) and on knowledge-based interpretation of medical images (e.g. [Tsuji and Nakao 1981]). Many of these papers contain information that is at least indirectly related to the domain of ground-level natural scenes.

The approach taken by Condor differs from previous efforts in that it includes:

- explicit representation and use of contextual information throughout the recognition process

- recognition in the absence of explicit shape description

- a limited search space, as a result of the context-based orientation

but avoids:

- reliance on accurately partitioned and delineated objects

- requirement for logically consistent absolute constraints

- use of probabilistic models requiring *a priori* probability values and independence assumptions.

The combination of these features makes Condor unique among computer vision systems.

2.3   Limitations of current machine-vision technology

The realization of robust recognition in the natural outdoor world will require that four current limitations of machine vision be overcome:

- The almost exclusive reliance upon shape

- The ill-defined nature of the partitioning problem

- The lack of an effective way to use context

- The inability to control the growth and complexity of the recognition search space.

These four obstacles must be overcome if machine recognition is to be possible in any complex domain. A domain can be considered complex for purposes of recognition if it exhibits some combination of the following properties: objects of interest do not have unique shapes; photometric appearance varies among individuals in a class; the vocabulary needed to describe the domain is open-ended; three-dimensional objects exist at all scales; and recognition involves a solution space that is too large to be searched completely. Examples of recognition domains that meet these complexity criteria are natural ground-level scene analysis, human face recognition, and medical image interpretation.

2.3.1   SHAPE

In most existing approaches to machine recognition, the shape of an object or of its parts has been the central issue. Indeed, many artifacts of human technology can be recognized solely on the basis of shape, which, to a large degree, accounts for the limited success so far achieved by machine recognition systems. These techniques cannot be extended to the natural world because shape alone is insufficient (even for people) to recognize most objects of interest (e.g., a rock or a river). It is easy to recognize a line drawing of an isolated telephone, but, as previously discussed, it is doubtful that one could correctly classify a river based entirely upon edges extracted from an image (Figure 2.1). Indeed, most natural objects fail this line drawing test, which requires identification based solely on observed shape. Similarly, when resolution is too coarse to discern shape, recognition is often

(a) Sobel edges from an image of a telephone

(b) Sobel edges from the image shown in Figure 1.1

FIGURE 2.1. Recognition by shape: The telephone is recognizable from edges extracted from an image, but the river is not.

possible on the basis of size and context. Marr [1982] has proposed the existence of a geometric surface description, known as the 2.5D sketch, as a significant intermediate representation in image understanding. While it is undeniably important in recognition of many objects, the 2.5D sketch is nearly meaningless for a tree. The fact that few natural objects have compact shape descriptions further complicates the use of shape in describing natural scenes. Thus a rather complex and cumbersome description would be required to describe the shape of something as common as a tree or a bush. It is obvious that shape cannot be the sole basis for a general-purpose recognition system.

2.3.2 UNIVERSAL PARTITIONING

A common paradigm in machine vision has been to partition an image into distinct regions that are uniform in intensity, texture, or some other easily computed attribute, and then assign labels to each such region. For natural scenes, however, it is seldom possible to establish complete boundaries between objects of interest. Consider the difficulty of associating leaves with their correct trees. Other examples are abundant: Where does a trunk end and a branch begin? What are the boundaries of a forest? Is a partially exposed root part of the ground or the tree?

Figure 2.2 shows a natural image that has been partitioned by a standard segmentation algorithm with several parameter settings using intensity and texture data simultaneously. The resulting map is of questionable utility for recognition regardless of the choice of parameters.

The reliance upon universal image partitioning algorithms in machine vision is surprising, given the abundance of evidence against their use by biological vision systems. Treisman has shown that the human visual system does not compute boundaries on the basis of any particular set of attributes [Treisman 1985]. She suggests that

> ... the preattentive visual system does not produce a single representation such as a single partitioned image. Rather, it provides different initial partitions to support distinct channels in the human visual system, which analyze imagery along a number of separate dimensions to extract such information as depth, movement, color, orientation, and so on. [Fischler and Firschein 1987b, p. 170].

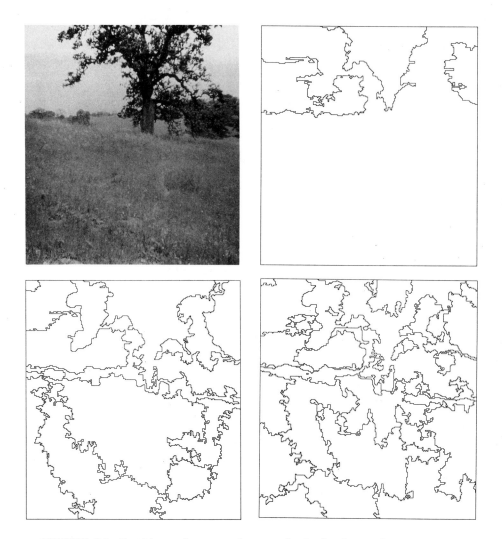

FIGURE 2.2. Partitions of a natural scene obtained using various parameter settings.

Image partitioning is also dependent upon its intended use. In an experiment in which subjects were asked to partition a curve into five segments, qualitatively different points were chosen depending on the objective conveyed to the subjects [Fischler and Bolles 1986, p. 100]. Fischler and Bolles concluded "Thus, even in the case of data with almost no semantic content, the partitioning problem is NOT a generic task independent of purpose."

Despite these difficulties, it remains necessary to perform some form of partitioning to do recognition, otherwise we have nothing to refer to when making a classification. Because of the impossibility of partitioning natural scenes reliably (even if such a goal were well-defined), we cannot rely on partitioning in the usual sense. Instead, we need an alternative view that allows object recognition without requiring complete or precise object delineation.

2.3.3 CONTEXTUAL KNOWLEDGE

It is widely known that an object's setting can strongly influence how that object is recognized, what it is recognized as, and if it is recognizable at all. Psychological studies have shown that people cannot understand a scene in the absence of sufficient context, yet when such contextual information is present, recognition is unequivocal [Fischler and Firschein 1987a, pp. 220–229]. Very little can be recognized when a scene is viewed through a small window or peephole. Furthermore, individual objects may exhibit a multitude of appearances under different imaging conditions, and many different objects may have the same image appearance. Their correct interpretation must be decided entirely by context. From these studies it is clear that computational vision systems will be unable to classify an object competently using only local information.

A perceptual system must have the ability to represent and use non-local information, to access a large store of knowledge about the geometric and physical properties of the world, and to use that information in the course of recognition. However, the few computational vision systems that make use of context do so superficially or in severely restricted ways. For example, Hawkeye used the location of a pier (obtained from a stored map of a port facility) to constrain the regions where a ship might be found [Barrow et. al. 1977]. SPAM used a map and domain-specific knowledge to find features in aerial imagery of airports [McKeown, Harvey, and McDermott 1985].

Of course, context is not necessary for everything. Many artifacts and some natural objects, such as a bird or a pine cone, can be instantly recognized even when all contextual clues have been removed. It is also possible to recognize some scenes in which contextual constraints have been violated. An image of an office scene with a telephone on the floor is unusual but not impossible to recognize. An image turned sideways is instantly recognized as such, despite the fact that relevant contextual knowledge is violated.

In natural scenes, however, contextual constraints are strong, and are less likely to be violated than in artificial scenes. In our work, we make the use of contextual information a central issue, and explicitly design a system to identify and use context as an integral part of recognition.

2.3.4 COMPUTATIONAL COMPLEXITY

The standard control structures currently employed in scene analysis lack an essential attribute of intelligent behavior — an explicit mechanism for generating a solution without requiring some form of combinatoric search. In controlled or simple environments, exhaustive search may be computationally feasible, but the complexity of the natural world imposes the requirement for a more direct solution mechanism. A key aspect of our approach is the provision of an explicit mechanism for generating high-quality assertions about the scene without the need for searching the exponential space of potential labels associated with image regions. Instead, we search the space of potential regions for each label, a space that is smaller because of the use of context to limit region generation. The customary region-oriented approach based on universal partitioning is exponential in the number of classes, which casts serious doubt on whether large-scale systems can be derived on that basis.

2.4   Key ideas

This section outlines the intuition behind our design for context-based vision. Chapter 4 provides a more formal description of the approach.

2.4.1 CONTEXT-LIMITED VISION

General-purpose machine vision is difficult — indeed, it seems impossible to many of us who have studied it. In fact, completely duplicating the human ability to recognize objects is probably equivalent to duplicating human intelligence. Nevertheless, it has been possible to attain a fair level of competence for machine vision systems in many important domains (e.g., optical character recognition, printed-circuit board inspection, industrial part positioning, and aerial-survey land-use classification). The common aspect of domains in which success has been achieved is the limited variability within the domain. In optical character recognition, fewer than 100 characters are usually considered and they occur in predictable locations. In industrial part positioning, there are only a few objects, and these have exactly the shapes specified in computer-aided design (CAD) models.

What prevents successful machine vision in more complex domains, such as the natural outdoor world or human face recognition, is the infinite variety of shapes and appearances that must be considered. When that variety is reduced, by searching for a particular tree in a particular image, or distinguishing just two human faces, the problem becomes far simpler. This observation can be summarized as the

> **Principle of Contextual Simplicity:** Within   any   given image, there is usually a relatively straightforward technique that will find the object or feature of interest.

Of course, that particular technique is likely to fail when used out of context, but if an appropriate context for its use can be found, successful recognition in a complex domain is possible. For example, the trees in Figure 2.3 can be isolated simply by thresholding the output of a texture operator. Employing the texture operator only where a tree is likely to be silhouetted against the sky allows some trees to be identified. Applying this operator out of context (e.g., below the skyline) is likely to produce a meaningless result.

In Condor we associate a data structure, called a *context set*, with each operator. The context set identifies those conditions that must be true for that operator to be applicable. Context sets can incorporate many kinds of contextual information including very general ("hilly terrain"), domain-specific ("under a palm tree"), image-specific ("silhouetted against the sky"), and instance-specific ("next to the Lone Cypress Tree"). Efficient

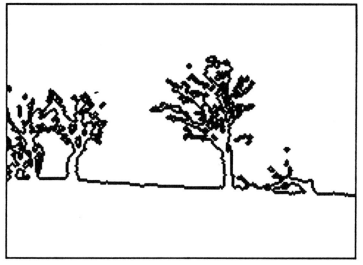

FIGURE 2.3. Some trees that can be delineated by a simple texture operator.

visual recognition can be achieved by invoking visual operations only in those contexts in which they are likely to succeed. Context sets and their design considerations are discussed in detail in Chapters 3 through 5.

2.4.2 GLOBAL CONSISTENCY

Even when the context associated with an operation is satisfied, the results may not be correct. Simple techniques are going to make mistakes, even in constrained contexts. Therefore, a means to verify the output of the various operators is required. This goal is accomplished through the application of the

> **Principle of Global Coherence:** The best interpretation of an image is the one that coherently explains the greatest portion of the sensed data.

The rationale behind this principle is the fact that a correct and complete interpretation should be entirely self-consistent and should explain the entire image. In practice, this ideal may not be realized, but the best interpretation ought to be the one that comes closest. Nothing is considered to be recognized unless it exists in the largest consistent set of hypotheses.

Traces of this strategy can be found in many places, including Waltz [Waltz 1972], SPAM [McKeown, Harvey, and McDermott 1985] and Hwang [Hwang 1984]. McKeown *et al.* recognized the value of mutual consistency among partial interpretations of airport scenes. Hwang grouped large numbers of potential hypotheses into consistent interpretations of suburban house scenes.

The principle demands *global* consistency because local constraints are not sufficient. The impossible object pictured in Figure 2.4 is an image that is locally consistent, but lacks a global interpretation. Such an image would be erroneously labeled by a system that used only local consistency checks, but is rejected by the Principle of Global Coherence.

A notion of consistency must be defined in order to make use of the Principle of Global Coherence. Many possibilities exist: neighboring region compatibility, image constraints, 3D occupancy, and so on. We have chosen to employ three-dimensional consistency because the constraints of the visual world are more naturally expressed that way. Many constraints that are easy to express with a 3D representation are difficult or impossible to express with a 2D (image plane) representation. For ex-

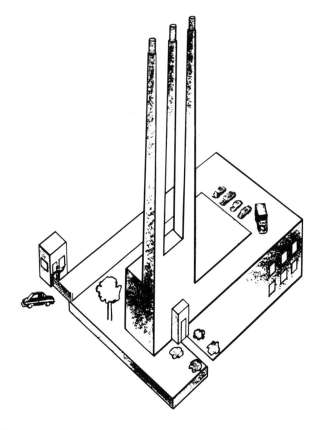

FIGURE 2.4. An impossible scene: no globally consistent interpretation exists.

ample, restrictions on size, distance, orientation, and physical support are all inherently 3D constraints. To attempt to define them as 2D constraints in the image plane would require the manipulation of projection artifacts such as occlusion, foreshortening, and perspective distortion. Other authors have also recommended the expression of constraints in 3D coordinate systems [McKeown, Harvey, and McDermott 1985, Jain 1989], and we strongly concur with that view.

Consistency constraints are represented by another form of context set. Each constraint is a predicate that can be used to decide if a candidate is consistent within a group of candidates. A context set specifies the conditions that must be true for that predicate to be appropriately applied.

2.4.3   CANDIDATE COMPARISON TO CONTROL COMPLEXITY

The Principle of Contextual Simplicity is used to generate candidate interpretations of parts of an image. The Principle of Global Coherence is used to determine the best interpretation of an entire image. However, the search for the largest coherent set of candidates can be combinatorically infeasible without further constraint. For this reason, mutually consistent sets of candidates (called *cliques*) are generated in a special order. The following principle allows cliques to be constructed such that the best cliques are generated early in the search:

> **Principle of Relative Recognition:** Given an image feature, it is often possible to determine whether it is a more likely example of a given class than another feature — even when it is impossible to make an absolute determination of class membership.

Consider the difficulty of assigning a label to a group of pixels in an image. Image information is unlikely to be sufficient for making a categorical determination of the region's identity. However, given two image regions, it is frequently easy to decide which is a better example of a specified class. This observation can be used to advantage when searching for mutually coherent sets of candidate hypotheses. Only when a sufficiently large and consistent clique is found is a final labeling assignment made.

At any point during the processing of an image, there will be a collection of candidates for each semantic category. Some of these candidates are obviously better examples of a given labeled class than others. The

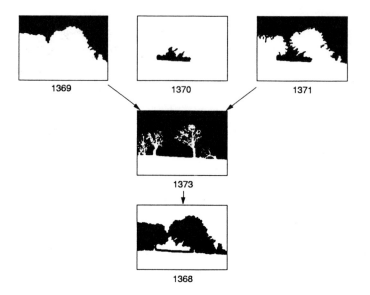

FIGURE 2.5. A collection of sky candidates that were generated by Condor.

candidates for each class can be compared pairwise to find those that are
most likely to be instances of the label, and, therefore, are most likely to
be present in the best (largest consistent) interpretation of the image. For
example, Figure 2.5 shows several candidates for the label "sky" from the
image shown in Figure 2.3. Region 1373 is a better example of sky than
Region 1368 because it is brighter and less textured.

Once again, the context set is the representation employed to encode
the criteria for comparison. These context sets contain a set of conditions
under which one candidate can be considered better than another as an instance of a particular label. When all these conditions favor one candidate
over the other, a preference ordering is established betwen them. When
there is disagreement among the context sets, the candidates are left unordered. Application of all such context sets imposes a partial order on the
candidates for each label.

These partial orders are then used when forming cliques of mutually
consistent candidates. The candidates at the top of a partial order are
tested for consistency with a clique before those candidates lower in the

order. This increases the chance that the largest consistent clique will be found early in the search because it increases the likelihood that a consistent candidate will be added to a clique.

The usual paradigm for scene interpretation is to pose the labeling of a partitioned image as a search problem — to find the best assignment of labels to regions in the space of all possible labelings [Yakimovsky and Feldman 1973, Barrow and Tenenbaum 1976]. To focus on search efficiency would be misdirected. If a search space is very large, no search method will succeed. If a search space is small, the method used doesn't matter. Therefore, a key to successful recognition is the restructuring of the usual paradigm to induce a smaller search space. In Condor, the search problem is inverted: the goal is to find the largest consistent collection of regions for the set of relevant labels. The context-based generation of candidate regions limits the size of the search space. The partial orders imposed by candidate comparison are a powerful tool for ordering the search through the space of mutually consistent cliques. Together, these two mechanisms avoid the combinatorics that prevent traditional techniques from achieving successful recognition in complex domains.

2.4.4 LAYERED PARTITIONS

Regardless of how it is derived, the final interpretation in most recognition systems is a labeled, partitioned image. In our approach, the final interpretation is a (maximal) clique of mutually consistent labeled regions. These regions will not be disjoint in general (may overlap) and may not cover the entire image. The clique can thus be viewed as a *layered partition*, where each layer is separated from others by the occlusion relations that have been determined during clique formation. Using the image shown in Figure 2.6, the difference between an ordinary partition and a layered partition is illustrated in Figure 2.7. As can be seen, the layered partition need not assign every pixel to a region, nor does it need to assign each pixel to only one region.

The layered partition has these advantages over the ordinary partition:

- Ambiguous pixels can be represented explicitly. For example, some pixels in the tree crown may be indistinguishable as sky or foliage. The layered partition allows those pixels to occur in regions for both sky and foliage.

FIGURE 2.6. A representative image of sparsely scattered trees.

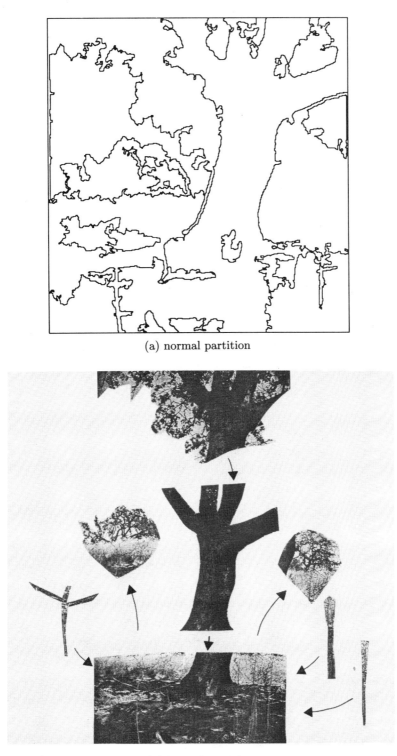

(a) normal partition

(b) layered partition

FIGURE 2.7. An ordinary partition vs. a layered partition.

- Occlusion relations are readily determined from the layered partition. For example, the thin weeds are in front of the large ground region and therefore must partially occlude it. No such relationship can be inferred from an ordinary partition.

- Coherent objects are represented as single units in the layered partition. In the ordinary partition, the ground has been split into several separate pieces and the relation among them has been lost. The layered partition, in which the ground is a single region, is more useful for performing higher-level reasoning about the scene content.

Thus in our approach, no single partitioning is created that supposedly describes the best segmentation of a scene. Rather, the layered partition is a flexible representation that is much in the spirit of the multiple partitions that Treisman found useful for describing human perception.

2.5   Experimental results

The ideas that we have proposed for overcoming the fundamental limitations of traditional approaches to machine vision have inspired the design of a complete architecture for visual recognition in complex domains. The adequacy of the approach is largely an empirical question that we address experimentally, using real imagery. The implementation of this architecture, known as Condor, has been used to assess the merits and limitations of the approach.

We have carried out extensive experimentation using Condor in the domain of ground-level views of natural scenes. Figure 2.6 depicts one of several hundred images that have been acquired from an undeveloped hilly region at Stanford University. A database of road networks and forested areas which is used by Condor as initial context has been manually constructed from the map in Figure 2.8. A digital terrain elevation model acquired from the United States Geological Survey is also stored in the world model. A knowledge base of 156 context sets tailored to this 2-square-mile region has been constructed and is used in our experimentation.

Images were acquired using a 35-mm stereo camera and then digitized, some in color and some as stereo pairs. Figure 2.9 illustrates the process of candidate generation using various operators on the image shown in Figure 2.6. The resulting hypotheses are compared pairwise to identify the

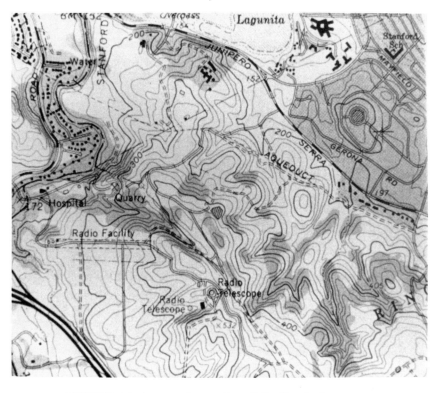

FIGURE 2.8. A map of a portion of the Stanford campus.

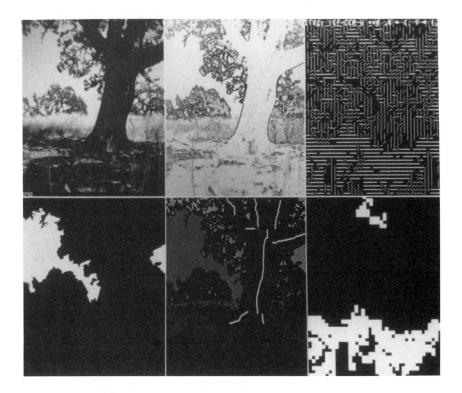

(a) Black-and-white image of some trees near Stanford	(b) Homogeneity operator — Each pixel value is the maximum difference in intensity between it and all neighboring pixels.	(c) Striations operator — Line segments show the orientation of any texture pattern in a small window.
(d) Sky region hypotheses – The entire scene was partitioned by Laws' segmenter, KNIFE [Laws 1988]. Each region displayed is above the geometric horizon, relatively bright, and relatively untextured.	(e) Tree trunk hypotheses — Coherent regions were grown from the output of the homogeneity operator (b) above. Skeletons of the major regions were constructed and filtered to remove short and highly convoluted skeletons. The tree trunk and its major limbs have been identified.	(f) Ground region hypotheses — Regions of horizontal striations were extracted from (c) above. Horizontal surfaces tend to have horizontal striations when viewed from an oblique angle due to perspective foreshortening.

FIGURE 2.9. Output of various operators applied to a natural scene.

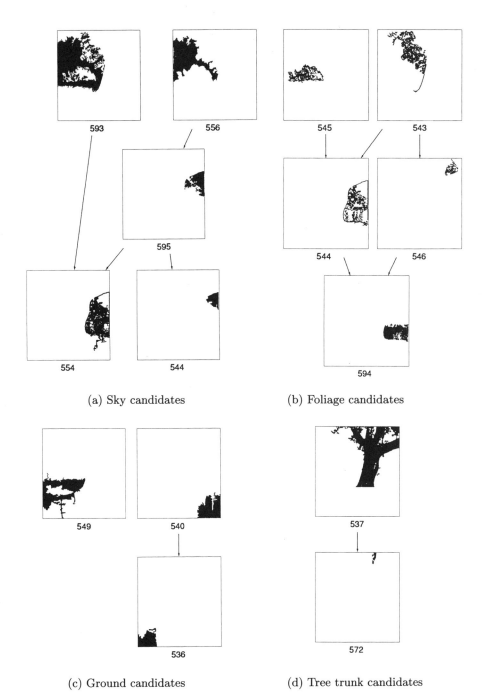

(a) Sky candidates

(b) Foliage candidates

(c) Ground candidates

(d) Tree trunk candidates

FIGURE 2.10. Partial orders of candidates.

(a)

(b)

FIGURE 2.11. Region coverage maps for two cliques formed by analyzing the tree image shown in Figure 2.6.

best candidates for each semantic label. The partial orders assembled for sky, foliage, ground, and tree-trunk are shown in Figure 2.10. Notice that there is no single partitioning — many candidates overlap each other and some pixels are left unexplained. While it would be nearly impossible to determine valid candidates in an absolute sense, the relative comparisons have correctly ranked good candidates above poor ones. Before making a final determination, Condor constructs cliques of mutually consistent candidates. The portion of the image included in the first two cliques is depicted in Figure 2.11. Although the labels are not shown in the figure, Clique (a) mistakenly labeled as sky the area below the foliage on the left. This prevented a large portion of the ground from being identified, so that it remained unlabeled. Clique (b) correctly labeled the area below the foliage as ground, and accordingly was able to find other ground candidates consistent with it. Clique (b) explains the larger portion of the image and the layered partition comprising it is preferred as the final interpretation. The tree and bushes identified in Clique (b) are added to the terrain database to be used as context for analyzing future images. A synthetic view of the contents of the updated world model is depicted in Figure 2.12.

Knowledge of the approximate position, size, shape, and appearance of a tree, for example, enables Condor to more competently extract that tree in another image by employing suitable procedures with appropriate parameter settings. In this way, Condor bootstraps its recognition abilities. When first introduced to an area, Condor knows only the topography and some gross features such as roads and forests. As Condor recognizes each new tree, bush, trail or other feature using generic operations, it adds to the context that is available for analyzing successive imagery. Eventually, a fairly complete, semantically labeled, 3D model of the environment is attained, which enables relatively rapid and reliable recognition of natural features in ground-level imagery using more specialized operators. To summarize, starting with a sparsely populated database of major terrain features, Condor learns a detailed description of the terrain, and learns how to recognize natural objects in a limited geographic area.

Using digitized images, we have performed numerous experiments demonstrating this behavior. In one set of experiments, Condor is tasked to analyze an image and to reanalyze it after updating the world model with its recognition results. On the first pass, Condor rarely mislabeled an object but often left a significant feature unlabeled. In some cases, the ad-

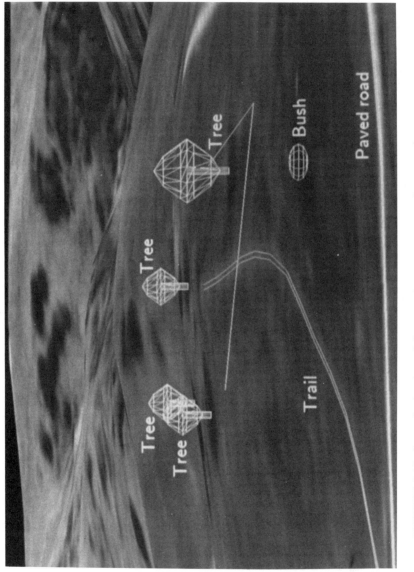

FIGURE 2.12. A synthetic view of the experimentation area after updating the world model.

ditional context provided from a partial recognition result allowed Condor
to recognize features on the second pass that were not identified on the
first.

In a second experiment, Condor is presented with a sequence of up to
eight images that might be obtained from a vehicle on a cross-country
traverse. By incrementally updating the world model, Condor recognizes
some features in the sequence that it was unable to recognize in the images
individually.

Other experiments have been performed using imagery widely separated
in time and in viewing direction. Numerous tests show that the prior context is responsible for recognition of new features (using newly satisfied context sets with more focused procedures); or makes recognition faster (fewer
cliques need to be constructed). In some cases, recognition was slower because additional procedures were applied that happened to be of no help.
There has not yet been a case in which the additional context prevented
recognition of a feature.

The experiments conducted led to the following conclusions:

- The Condor architecture can reliably recognize natural features in
  images from the environment for which its knowledge base was constructed.

- The contextual information stored in the world model is essential for
  the recognition of some features.

- The system can learn to recognize objects in a limited geographic area
  by storing partial recognition results and using them as contextual
  information.

2.6 Conclusions

An autonomous vehicle that is to operate intelligently in a nontailored environment must have the ability to recognize the objects it encounters. Navigation, task execution, and planning all require a semantic understanding
of the environment that is not available in a geometric representation, no
matter how precise. Visual recognition is indispensable for an autonomous
system, but no existing approaches are competent to provide recognition
in complex domains.

We have identified four fundamental obstacles that have hindered efforts to construct a viable system for visual recognition in the natural world:

- Geometric models alone are insufficient for recognizing objects in complex domains.

- Image partitioning, as traditionally defined, is not able to accomplish its intended purpose — a universal decomposition of an image into semantically meaningful regions.

- Contextual information cannot be represented or exploited effectively in conventional scene-understanding systems.

- Exhaustive search is not feasible in complex domains, but conventional vision systems have no mechanisms for avoiding exponential growth in search time as the recognition vocabulary increases.

Several ideas are described that offer partial solutions to these problems.

The use of a multiplicity of simple techniques in constrained contexts produces recognition tactics that can take advantage of appearance, setting, and purpose, as well as shape. Context sets are used to represent those conditions that should be satisfied for a particular operation to be meaningful. Thus, there is no need to rely on shape as the primary recognition cue, and the use of contextual information is embedded uniformly into every level of the system.

In a departure from the usual practice of complete image partitioning, there is no need to segment an image before interpreting it. Instead, a layered partition is produced as a result of image interpretation.

The insistence on global coherence among all candidates in a clique is the key to achieving reliable recognition, even when the individual operations are fallible. Construction of partial orderings before nominating candidates to a clique reduces the combinatorics that otherwise would inhibit consistency checking. Together, these ideas allow robust recognition in a computationally feasible paradigm.

In this chapter a number of ideas have been expressed that can serve as ingredients of a realistic system for natural object recognition. In succeeding chapters, these ingredients are molded together into a complete strategy designed to achieve robust recognition in complex domains by exploiting contextual information.

3

A VISION SYSTEM FOR OFF-ROAD NAVIGATION

Rather than study natural object recognition in the abstract, we have chosen to focus our research on the visual requirements of a particular task. Evaluation of the merits of any approach or theory can be carried out only within the scope of an intended purpose. Natural object recognition is too broad and ill-defined to serve as a useful goal for machine vision unless a task is chosen that allows the accomplishments of various approaches to be measured. Further, in defining the task we constrain the breadth of capabilities that must be developed before a practical contribution is attained and we establish a concrete foundation that can be referred to when design decisions are to be made.

3.1 Task scenario

An autonomous ground vehicle is to operate in a natural outdoor environment of limited geographic extent. Its ultimate task may be anything from cattle herding to military surveillance, but our primary concern will be to endow it with the ability to recognize features useful for navigation.

Such a vehicle cannot rely entirely upon a range sensor for obstacle avoidance if it is to navigate intelligently. Simply avoiding every obstruction detected by a range sensor is wasteful — why go around a small bush when the vehicle may proceed safely over it? Worse, this avoidance strategy may force the vehicle to conclude that there is no safe path from its present location to its goal when in fact there may be many. An intelligent vehicle must have the ability to discriminate between a bush and a rock, between a tall weed and a rigid pipe, between a pile of leaves and a tree stump. Additionally, the range sensor will fail to detect some features that pose true obstacles to the vehicle. To a rangefinder, an impassable muddy road appears the same as a dry one, a marsh and a grassy field may be indistinguishable, and a lake may look like a parking lot. It is probably not wise to risk the well-being of an autonomous vehicle without reducing these hazards.

Recognizing some of these obstacles through tactile sensing may be possible but could impose significant demands on the vehicle in terms of weight, power, maximum safe speed, and modes of operation. Visual recognition of these and other obstacles seems more desirable and may be feasible based on the results presented here.

When the vehicle is first introduced into an area, it will have little or no understanding of the geographic arrangement or appearance of the features it will encounter. Before being released to carry out its intended mission, the vehicle will undertake an exploration of the environment. During the initial exploration, the vehicle will collect and analyze imagery, storing the results in a geographic database. There is no need for this to occur in real time — it may even be desirable for the vehicle to interpret its imagery overnight. The goal is to store sufficient information about each object so that it or a similar object will be recognized when seen again.

After the exploration phase has been conducted, the vehicle will begin its mission-oriented work. The information gleaned from its prior experience should enable it to reliably identify the natural features it encounters. Ideally, this will allow the vehicle to operate safely and to plan its actions intelligently based on knowledge of its environment.

3.2   Prior knowledge

A vehicle operating within the scenario just described has the possibility of making use of a substantial collection of information that could help it perform object recognition. Whereas early attempts at natural scene recognition were conducted in the absence of such a context, our approach is explicitly designed to make maximum use of any information that might be available to a vision system employed on a real vehicle. Doing so is one of the factors that has made it possible to solve what might otherwise be an intractable problem.

A vehicle-mounted vision system has access to information that is inherent in the scenario as well as that provided by on-board sensors. This information includes both image-specific and scene-specific knowledge. The following pieces of information are presumed to be available to an autonomous vehicle and are used by Condor when interpreting an image:

- Camera position — The position of the vehicle can be provided by some combination of an inertial navigation system (INS), dead reckoning, a Global Positioning System (GPS), and landmark recognition. GPS alone can locate a moving vehicle within 5 meters in real time. Better accuracy can be achieved by combining several positioning techniques, although it is unrealistic to expect arbitrary precision. The camera is assumed to be rigidly mounted to the vehicle; therefore, its position in the world is known given the position and orientation of the vehicle.

- Camera orientation — The orientation of the vehicle is provided in three degrees of freedom by INS or other sensors. The orientation of the camera relative to the vehicle is either fixed or measured by internal sensors.

- Focal length — The focal length of the camera is assumed to be fixed and therefore known.

- Principal point — The principal point is the intersection of the optical axis with the film plane, and is calibrated before employment of the vehicle. The vision system is informed if the images it is presented with have been cropped or scaled.

- Geometric horizon — The geometric horizon is the line in the image where the skyline would appear if the world were flat and level. The geometric horizon constrains the scene (for example, the true skyline cannot be below it), and is easily computed from knowledge of the camera orientation.

- Time and date — The sun's position (and the moon's position and phase) can be computed from knowledge of the vehicle's position, the date, and the time. These objects, if visible in an image, can be recognized by verification. The sun position can be used for shadow prediction.

Because the vehicle is operating in a limited geographic area, there is a permanence to many of the features it will encounter. How to represent and exploit this information for object recognition has been one of our primary research issues. We find it reasonable to provide Condor with the following information about the region:

- Generic knowledge — Just as a rabbit "knows," for example, that trees have branches, the vehicle should have access to this type of knowledge as well. Some such knowledge may be only locally generic, such as the fact that there are oak trees in the area of operation.

- Topography — Digital terrain elevation data (DTED) are available from the United States Geological Survey and from the Defense Mapping Agency. The resolution is coarse by ground vehicle standards (30 meter grid), but is of some use in scene interpretation. Additional elevation data can be obtained from aerial imagery by stereopsis [Barnard and Fischler 1982] for regions and resolutions not otherwise available.

- Map data — High-resolution maps exist for nearly every region on earth. This information can be provided in a geographic database (digitized manually if necessary). The resolution will not be sufficient for navigation, but the data should be useful for ground-level image interpretation.

Some other pieces of knowledge may be sufficiently static that one could provide them to the vehicle on a periodic basis (during vehicle maintenance, for example):

- Weather — The cloud conditions and precipitation can have a large effect on image appearance. Periodically providing weather updates (or predictions) should be useful for image interpretation.

- Appearance of distant objects — A faraway object, such as a mountain range, has a constant appearance when viewed from anywhere within a sufficiently small area. Manual identification of a mountain range should enable a vision system to recognize it when seen again later.

Access to prior information is potentially valuable, but actually worthless without a means to exploit it. The ability to make use of prior knowledge using context sets is one of the primary attributes separating Condor from other research aimed at natural object recognition.

TABLE 3.1. Accuracy of several range-finding systems.

	Range		
Source	10 meters	30 meters	100 meters
Human vision	0.20 m	1.5 m	25 m
Binocular stereo	0.10 m	0.7 m	10 m
ERIM laser scanner	0.12 m	0.9 m	4 m

3.3 The role of geometry

Although our approach does not rely on geometric models of the objects of interest (in contrast to most approaches to object recognition), 3D geometry clearly plays an important role in image interpretation.

3.3.1 SOURCES AND LIMITATIONS OF RANGE DATA

Although humans have little trouble perceiving 3D structure in images of uncontrived scenes, computational vision systems lack the human ability to use semantic knowledge to recover geometry. Autonomous vehicles are likely to be equipped with laser rangefinders or stereo cameras to recover depth information, although even these forms of direct sensing have severe limitations. Table 3.1 shows the range resolution attainable by the latest ERIM laser rangefinder, by a typical binocular stereo setup for a ground vehicle application,[1] and by the human visual system in the absence of semantic cues. In all three cases, the error associated with depth measurements increases with the square of the distance; clearly, one cannot rely upon 3D shape as the primary basis for recognition of anything but nearby objects.

Our context-based approach is designed to make use of range data when they are available, and to proceed without them otherwise. Performance and competence are degraded in the absence of range data, but substantial recognition abilities are retained.

Our current implementation of Condor, which is concerned with identifying macroscopic features such as trees, bushes, and rocks, makes quantitative use of range data only for objects within 10 meters of the vehicle.

---

[1]The binocular stereo computation assumes a 60-degree field of view, a 512 x 512 pixel image, and a baseline of 2 meters.

Range data out to 100 meters are used qualitatively (e.g. for rough estimates of the size of a tree or its placement in the world). Beyond 100 meters, the range data are ignored as being too unreliable for productive use. It is interesting to note that human stereoscopic capabilities are no better than current electronic sensors — people rely on a host of other cues for acquiring a 3D model of a scene [Cavanagh 1987]. Human binocular stereovision has limited use beyond arm's length.

When considering objects beyond 10 meters, or when range data are not available, Condor makes use of other cues for constraining the 3D interpretation of a scene:

- Size constraints — Once an object has been recognized (as a tree, for example), the natural limits on its size can be used to bound its distance from the camera. For example, if a tree region that subtends 20 degrees in the field of view were more than 300 meters away, it would have to be over 100 meters tall.

- Height in image — The natural world consists mainly of a support surface populated with raised objects. Except in the case of overhanging objects (such as branches), points higher in any image column are farther from the camera. This rule can be used to constrain the 3D placement of objects, after overhanging objects, which typically occur only in the foreground, have been identified.

- Ridge lines — When looking at hilly terrain, one finds that the ground recedes continuously except at ridge lines. Detecting these discontinuities provides information for ordering the depth of objects that appear on the ground.

- Striations — When viewing a natural scene at the highly oblique angles typical of a ground-based vehicle, one sees that the ground tends to appear horizontally striated because of the foreshortening of texture along the view direction. Our experiments reveal this to be true, even when tall grass is present. This phenomenon is extremely useful for detecting horizontal surfaces.

- Prior knowledge — Although the absolute distance to an object cannot be precisely determined even at moderate ranges, it is often possible to determine whether one object is nearer or farther than another.

If the position of a reference object is known (stored in the geographic database), the possible location of an unknown object is constrained.

Other cues to depth recovery are available, but have not been used in our research. Some cues worthy of additional consideration are optic flow; shape-from-shading and shape-from-texture (both of which might be feasible within the constrained contexts identified by Condor); occlusion boundaries, which permit a depth ordering between two surfaces; the texture gradient that occurs as a surface fades into the distance; and the bluing and whitening effects of the atmosphere on distant terrain.

3.3.2 USING THREE-DIMENSIONAL GEOMETRIC INFORMATION

Recovering the 3D layout of a scene is important not only for mission-related tasks such as navigation, but also for image interpretation. Constraints imposed by the 3D world can be used to detect inconsistent recognition hypotheses that could not be detected by 2D reasoning. Condor attempts to recover 3D information about a scene that is of value in image understanding.

We make no attempt to recover the precise shapes of the ground or objects in a scene. Geometric reconstruction has received considerable attention in the past decade and has produced some impressive results in special circumstances (for example [Barnard and Fischler 1982, Pentland 1986a, Baker and Bolles 1988, Horn 1989]). Our approach has been designed to make use of these results, but not to rely on them and not to attempt to duplicate them. Instead, the 3D geometric information that is recovered is used to predict the image location of an object and to establish geometric constraints such as existence of a support surface and proper balance.

The geometric container is subdivided into two parts reflecting the absolute and relative nature of geometric information. *Relative geometry* amounts to the relative depth relations among objects in an image, and is viewpoint-dependent. It is instantiated during image interpretation by the various cues listed in Section 3.3.1 and is expressed as a layered partition, in which each layer is more distant than some of the previous layers. These distance relations among image regions can be expressed as a depth lattice, by explicitly linking those objects whose depth ordering is known.

Absolute geometry involves those objects whose distance from the cam-

era is known with some precision. Because we assume that we always know
the location and orientation of the camera with reasonable accuracy, we
can compute the world location of these objects. We choose to store absolute geometric information in a world coordinate system for convenience.
The Core Knowledge Structure (CKS) is used as a geographic database
both for objects whose locations are known *a priori*, as well as for objects whose locations are hypothesized during image interpretation. Appendix A contains a brief description of the CKS [Smith and Strat 1986,
Strat and Smith 1987a]. The multiple-resolution facilities of the CKS allow
object locations to be specified with appropriate accuracy bounds.

Upon completion of the analysis of an image, the absolute geometric
information is posted in the geographic database to become available for
interpreting subsequent images. The relative geometric information is used
to place objects in the CKS in sizable uncertainty regions. For those objects
whose uncertainty regions are too large, the information is not stored in
the CKS and the relative geometry is lost.

3.4   A vocabulary for recognition

Object recognition involves the assignment of labels to image features. The
set of labels constitutes a vocabulary for describing a scene. Before one can
consider strategies for recognizing objects one must decide on the classes
of objects that are to be instantiated.

Unlike previous approaches, we differentiate between the target vocabulary and the recognition vocabulary. The *target vocabulary* is the set of
labels that one is ultimately interested in recognizing from imagery. The
recognition vocabulary contains the target vocabulary plus those additional
terms that may be of use in recognizing instances of the target vocabulary.

Human psychologists differentiate between primal or basic-level terms
and nonprimal or subordinate terms [Biederman 1988]. Basic-level terms
denote those classes of objects whose presence in an image can be decided
without deduction, presumably from features directly extracted from the
image. Recognition of subordinate terms first requires recognition of one
or more basic-level categories from which the presence of the subordinate
term is determined. Subordinate categories are not instantiated directly
from image features — for example, banana is a basic-level term while
fruit, a subordinate category, is not.

3.4.1 TARGET VOCABULARY

The target vocabulary is dictated by the task that the vision system is to perform. We have been concerned with navigation in the natural outdoor world. Accordingly, the appropriate target vocabulary includes terms such as bush, rock, ditch, grass, tree, cliff, stream, log, stump, sand, and so on. It would not be appropriate to include shadow, since shadow detection is not immediately useful for navigation. It may not be useful to include both oak tree and laurel tree, because the difference is probably not pertinent for the navigation task. Similarly, the scale of the task makes it unnecessary to include spider or paramecium.

The words included in the vocabulary are used only as labels for particular classes of objects. Many English words have multiple meanings — e.g., rock can denote either a single object or a type of matter. We are not concerned with linguistic disambiguation because the labels are chosen to name particular categories. Each vocabulary word is intended to denote a single category, and pseudo-words are coined when appropriate English words do not exist. We use a special font (as in **tree**) to distinguish vocabulary words from their English counterparts.

3.4.2 RECOGNITION VOCABULARY

Although **tree** is a member of the target vocabulary, it is probably not possible to detect a tree in an image directly. Rather, the presence of a tree is deduced from the recognition of a tree trunk and a tree crown in the proper spatial relationship. **Tree-crown** and **tree-trunk**, therefore, are included in the recognition vocabulary. Other classes, such as **horizon**, **skyline**, and **sky**, are of great value in interpreting ground-level natural scenes and are included as terms in the recognition vocabulary. Other terms are added as experience dictates. A semantic net showing a recognition vocabulary for the navigation task and the class containment hierarchy among those terms is depicted in Figure 3.1.

The terms that occur in the recognition vocabulary span a range of spatial scales and semantic abstraction levels. These two axes define a space of spatial and semantic resolution that provides insight into the roles that individual terms play. Several example terms from a recognition vocabulary are plotted in this resolution space in Figure 3.2. The abscissa shows increasing semantic precision from very generic physical and geometric properties

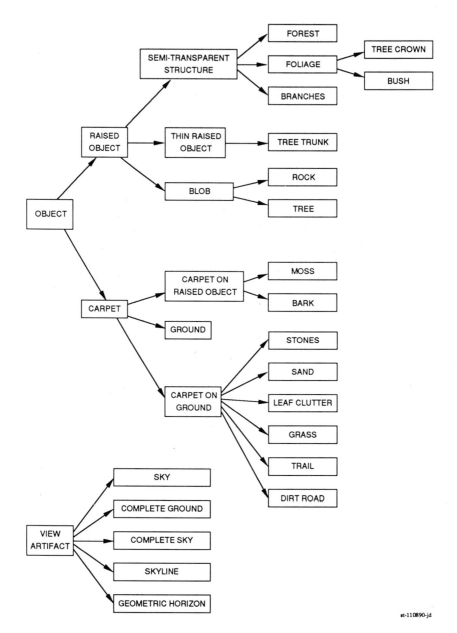

st-110890-jd

FIGURE 3.1. Abstraction hierarchy of terms in the recognition vocabulary.

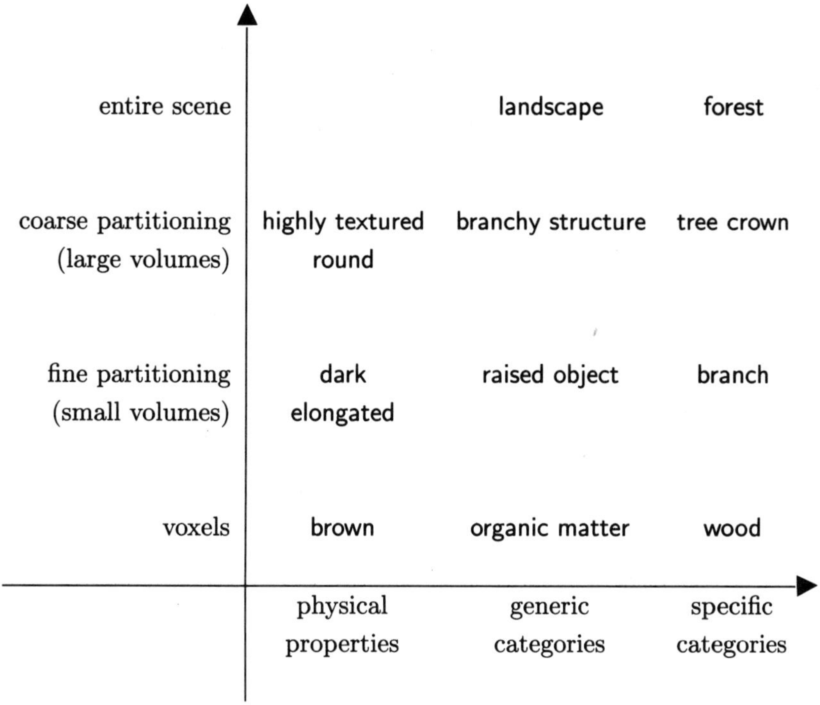

	physical properties	generic categories	specific categories
entire scene		landscape	forest
coarse partitioning (large volumes)	highly textured round	branchy structure	tree crown
fine partitioning (small volumes)	dark elongated	raised object	branch
voxels	brown	organic matter	wood

FIGURE 3.2. Axes of spatial and semantic resolution.

to rather specific semantically meaningful categories. The ordinate shows increasing spatial scale, from individual voxels, through finite volumes of increasing size, to an entire scene. While the target vocabulary consists primarily of terms near the right edge of the diagram, image interpretation involves instantiating image features at the full range of spatial and semantic scales.

3.5   Contextual information

We have already observed that contextual information is of great potential value for visual recognition of objects, particularly in natural scenes. The difficulty lies in devising an effective mechanism for exploiting context. Our solution to this problem is presented in Chapter 4, where we describe a computational architecture that has been constructed for the express purpose of bringing contextual information to bear at all levels of the visual recognition task.

The scale of contextual information is an important issue. A completely labeled scene is a form of context, but one that is impractical to provide. A tradeoff exists between the resolution of contextual information and its utility for recognition. A very specific context facilitates visual recognition, but will seldom be applicable (and therefore would be costly to provide in sufficient numbers). A generic context can be used often, but is less powerful in its constraints for recognition routines. Finding the middle ground — the proper balance between specificity of context, utility for recognition, and frequency of occurrence — is the key to constructing suitable context sets for visual routines.

3.5.1   TYPES OF CONTEXT

Before discussing how context is to be used, it is important to assess what contextual information is available. In our case, this is dictated in part by the autonomous ground-vehicle scenario. Rather than attempt to define what we mean by context, we enumerate four broad categories of information that should impart the range of information that we wish to include in our concept of context:

- Photogrammetric context — information surrounding the acquisition of the image under study. This includes both internal camera parameters (e.g., focal length, principal point, field of view, color of filter) as well as external parameters (camera location and orientation). We also include the date and time of image acquistion as well as the images themselves.

- Physical context — information about the visual world that is independent of any particular set of image acquisition conditions. Physical context encompasses a range of specificity from the very precise "There is a tree at (342, 124)," to the more generic "This area contains a mixed, deciduous forest." Physical context may also include information about the appearance of scene features in previously interpreted imagery and dynamic information, such as weather conditions and seasonal variations.

- Hypothetical context — information about an image that is hypothesized during computation. Hypothetical context includes tentative conclusions such as "Region 943 is a bush" or "The skyline is not visible in this image." This permits hypothetical reasoning using partial results. Once an image is completely analyzed, any surviving hypotheses are stored in the geographic database and become physical context for use during the analysis of subsequent images.

- Computational context — information about the internal state of processing. The computational context can be used to control the processing sequence based on partial recognition results. Different strategies can be used when first initiating the analysis of an image versus filling in the details of a largely completed analysis.

These four categories of contextual information have been instantiated and have proved beneficial for natural object recognition. All contextual information is referenced uniformly using context sets; the subdivision of context into categories provides an organizing principle that is useful during the engineering of context sets.

3.5.2 USING CONTEXT

The value of explicitly representing and using context lies in the relative ease with which many features can be recognized in constrained contexts. The ultimate question of what elements of context to encode is determined by the task undertaken by the system and its associated recognition requirements.

In Condor, operations that can benefit from knowledge of context are the generation of candidate labeled-region hypotheses, evaluation of those hypotheses, and tests for mutual consistency. For instance, in the context of an image acquired from a horizontally aimed camera on a clear day, finding bright blue regions is a good way to generate candidates for sky. In the context of a foliage candidate silhouetted against the sky, strong texture is one reasonable evaluation metric. In the context of the hypothetical determination that the lower half of an image is clear ground, it would be inconsistent to label an overlapping region as tree-trunk.

The strategy that Condor employs is to determine as much contextual information as is likely to be useful for recognition. Some context is known in advance, by virtue of the fact that the visual system is situated in the world (as discussed in Section 3.2). Other elements of context are recognized through image analysis. Condor's behavior is to bootstrap its recognition abilities by first recognizing features that are easily distinguished, then using that information as context to constrain the recognition of more difficult features.

4

CONTEXT-BASED VISION

This chapter provides details of our context-driven approach to machine vision. It describes the Condor architecture, gives details of the algorithms embedded within it, and provides an example of its application to natural object recognition.

4.1 Conceptual Architecture

Condor has been designed to perform robust recognition in complex visual domains, such as ground-level scenes of the natural outdoor world. Its fundamental structure can be characterized as following the generate-evaluate-test paradigm found in many AI systems, although its use of context within that paradigm is unique.

4.1.1 OVERVIEW

In describing the architecture of the system, we differentiate between the conceptual architecture and the implementation of Condor. The conceptual architecture involves many parallel asynchronous operations that access a collection of shared knowledge. It has been inspired in part by psychophysical investigations of biological vision systems and is designed to have the potential to achieve equivalent recognition abilities. Many of its features have been included to assure highly reliable recognition without undue concern for efficient execution.

The architecture as actually implemented is necessarily concerned with computational efficiency. The architecture has been serialized to run on a conventional uniprocessor. Although Condor has demonstrated significant recognition abilities using a variety of ground-level imagery, the knowledge base certainly is not as complete as would be needed for the interpretation of arbitrary images from the domain.

The conceptual architecture of Condor is depicted in Figure 4.1. The

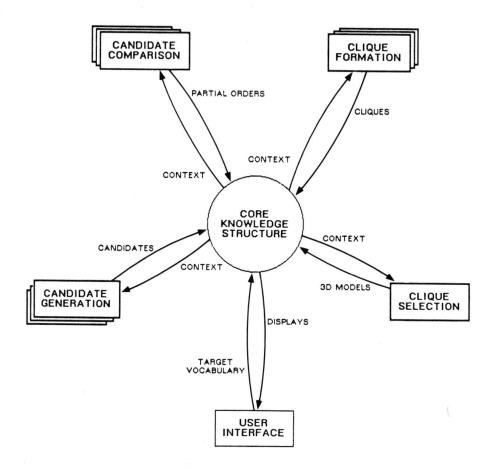

FIGURE 4.1. Conceptual architecture of Condor.

input to the system is an image or set of images that may include intensity, range, color, or other data modalities. The primary output of the system is a labeled 3D model of the scene. The labels included in the output description denote object *classes* (defined below) that the system has been tasked to recognize, plus others from the recognition vocabulary that happen to be found useful during the recognition process.

Definition 1: A *class*, denoted by L, is a category of scene features where L is one of the terms in the recognition vocabulary. That is,

$$L \in \text{RECOGNITION-VOCABULARY}.$$

Example:
$$L \in \{\text{sky, ground, geometric-horizon, foliage, bush,}$$
$$\text{tree-trunk, tree-crown, trail, ... }\}$$

A central component of the architecture is a special-purpose knowledge base/database used for storing and providing access to knowledge about the visual world, as well as tentative conclusions derived during operation of the system. In Condor, these capabilities are provided by the Core Knowledge Structure [Smith and Strat 1986, Strat and Smith 1987a].

The conceptual architecture is much like that of a blackboard system; there are many computational processes interacting through a shared data structure. Interpretation of an image involves the following four process types:

- Candidate generation

- Candidate comparison

- Clique formation

- Clique selection

Each process acts like a daemon, watching over the knowledge base and invoking itself when its contextual requirements are satisfied. All processing occurs asynchronously and each process is assumed to have access to sufficient computational resources. All processes have access to the entire knowledge base, but each type of process will store only the kind of information shown in the diagram (Figure 4.1).

4.1.2 CONTEXT SETS

The invocation of all processing operations in Condor is governed by context. Rather than hard-wire the control structure and control decisions to be made, the architecture is driven by context. All processing actions are controlled by context sets, and are invoked only when their context sets are satisfied. Thus, the actual sequence of computations (and the labeling decisions that are made) are dictated by contextual information, which is represented by the data stored in the Core Knowledge Structure, by the computational state of the system, and by the image data available for interpretation. Contextual information is referenced by the context sets, each of which is composed of some number of *context elements*, defined here.

Definition 2: A *context element, CE_i*, is a predicate involving any number of terms that refer to the photogrammetric, physical, hypothetical or computational context of image analysis.

Example: Some of the context elements employed by Condor are:

SKY-IS-CLEAR, CAMERA-IS-HORIZONTAL, LAST-CANDIDATE-IS(FOLIAGE) .

Definition 3: A context element CE_i is *satisfied* if and only if the known context is sufficient to establish the truth of the predicate.

Often it will not be possible to establish whether a context element is true or false, in which case the context element is considered to be unsatisfied.

Visual interpretation knowledge is encoded in *context sets*, which serve as the uniform knowledge representation scheme used throughout the system.

Definition 4: A *context set, CS_k*, is a collection of context elements that are sufficient for inferring some relation or carrying out some operation on an image.

Syntactically, a context set is embedded in a *context rule* denoted by

$$L : \{CE_1, CE_2, \cdots, CE_n\} \implies A$$

where L is the name of the class associated with the context set, A is an action to be performed, and the CE_i comprise a set of conditions that define a context.

Example: The context set

{SKY-IS-CLEAR, CAMERA-IS-HORIZONTAL, RGB-IS-AVAILABLE}

defines a set of conditions under which it is appropriate to use the operator **BLUE-REGIONS** to delineate candidate sky hypotheses.

There is a collection of context rules for every class in the recognition vocabulary. In theory, Condor performs the actions A that are associated with every *satisfied* context set.

Definition 5: A context set CS_k is *satisfied* if and only if all of its context elements CE_i are satisfied.

Context sets are employed in three varieties of rules:

- Type I — Candidate generation

- Type II — Candidate evaluation

- Type III — Consistency determination

Context rules of each type are constructed for each class in the recognition vocabulary. The most difficult part of building any AI system is encoding the knowledge that drives the system. Constructing context sets in Condor is tantamount to knowledge-base construction and remains a critical task requiring a solid understanding of the limitations and applicability conditions of potential image-understanding routines. Condor has been designed with this in mind, and offers several features that facilitate this process.

First, the construction task is eased somewhat by the separation of the knowledge base according to classes. Therefore, when the designer is constructing context rules for class L, the only other classes that must be considered are those that are immediately relevant for recognizing instances of class L.

Second, context sets need only define sufficient conditions for applying the associated operation — they need not attempt to define the full boundary of applicability. Thus, one can be quite conservative when constructing context sets, encoding only knowledge that is clearly relevant and ignoring knowledge that may be dubious.

Third, although it is desirable that the context sets and their associated operations be as infallible as possible, they need not be perfect. The entire architecture of Condor has been designed to achieve reliable recognition results, even in the presence of unreliable operators, imperfect evaluators, and faulty decision-makers. This is achieved primarily through the use of large numbers of redundant operations in every stage of processing, so that a single mistake is unlikely to affect the final interpretation.

Finally, some form of learning is essential if a large system with a broad range of competence is to be constructed. We have proposed a mechanism whereby context sets can be modified automatically, using the experiences of the system to refine the knowledge base incrementally. The collection of context sets can be allowed to evolve, with or without human intervention.

4.1.3   CANDIDATE GENERATION

The customary approach to recognition in machine vision is to design an analysis technique that is reliable in as many contexts as possible. In contrast to this tendency toward large, monolithic procedures, the strategy embodied in Condor is to make use of a large number of relatively simple procedures. Each procedure is competent only in some restricted context, but collectively, these procedures offer the potential to recognize a feature in a wide range of contexts. The key to making this strategy work is to use contextual information to predict which procedures are likely to yield desirable results, and which are not.

While it may be extremely difficult to write a recognition procedure that is competent across many different contexts, it is often quite easy to devise a procedure that works well in some specific context. For example, finding foliage that is silhouetted against the sky is far simpler than finding foliage in general. Similarly, finding foliage in an environment where only a single species of tree occurs is easier than finding foliage associated with any kind of tree. By assembling a collection of such context-specific procedures, it has been possible to recognize foliage in many different situations under a wide variety of conditions.

A collection of recognition procedures is associated with each class in the recognition vocabulary. Of course, no procedure, not even one applied in very restricted contexts, will be sufficiently reliable that its results can be accepted with confidence. Accordingly, the output of each procedure is treated as a *candidate* hypothesis.

Definition 6: A *candidate* is any image feature that is potentially an instance of some specified class L. Every candidate is associated with some class.

In most of our examples, an image region is associated with each candidate but, in general, a candidate is a hypothesis that asserts the presence of some object in the 3D scene depicted in the image being analyzed. Candidates are generated by specialized operators using either intensity or range data, and every candidate is associated with the class of which it is potentially an instance.

A large portion of the Condor architecture is devoted to sorting out the better candidate hypotheses from the poorer ones. Figure 4.2 shows the generation and subsequent processing of candidates throughout the system. The invocation of recognition procedures is governed by Type I context sets which define the conditions under which it is sensible to employ each recognition procedure.

Definition 7: Type I Context Rule — Candidate Generation:

$$L : \{CE_1, CE_2, \cdots, CE_n\} \implies A$$

If all context elements CE_i are satisfied, then A should be employed as an operator that will generate candidate hypotheses for instances of class L.

Example: The operator BLUE-REGIONS can be used to find sky candidates only when the camera is approximately horizontal, the sky is not cloudy, and color imagery is available:

$$\text{SKY} : \{\text{SKY-IS-CLEAR, CAMERA-IS-HORIZONTAL, RGB-IS-AVAILABLE}\}$$
$$\implies \text{BLUE-REGIONS} .$$

The context elements in a candidate generator context set encode the assumptions that were made when operator A was written. This formalism ensures that each operator will be employed only in circumstances in which it can reasonably be expected to succeed. The context set not only identifies an applicable procedure, but also supplies the information to establish intelligently the inevitable assumptions and parameters (such as a threshold or a window size) associated with that operator.

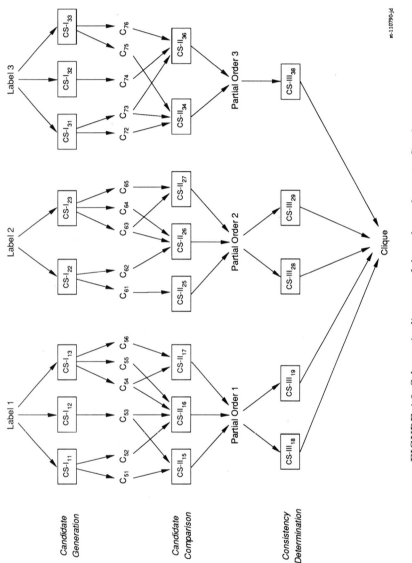

FIGURE 4.2. Schematic diagram of data dependence in Condor.

Obviously, context sets can be very specific, very generic, or anywhere in between. It is intended that candidate generator context sets be provided that span this range. One encodes highly specific context sets for operators that work well only in very special circumstances, presumably a context that has some special significance to the larger goals of the embedded system. Generic operators that provide reasonable performance over a broad range of contexts are employed when the more competent specialized procedures are not applicable. Generally, the more candidate generator context sets that are provided, the more operators that will be applicable in any given context. Ideally, there will always be multiple operators invoked so that the system need never rely on a single routine.

It should be clear that it is possible to make use of large, carefully constructed procedures when they exist. Thus, if one has already expended a great deal of effort tuning a large, monolithic recognition procedure, it can be incorporated into Condor alongside any other operators that might also exist.

The interaction of context sets across classes is of interest. The context elements in one context set may refer to the existence of other labeled entities. For example, a tree-trunk candidate-generation routine may require knowledge of the ground location as part of its context. Whenever a need for recognition of other classes is detected, Condor adds that class to its list of labels that are actively being recognized. In this way, when Condor is tasked to recognize a specific class from its target vocabulary, it will automatically seek to instantiate other relevant classes from its recognition vocabulary.

4.1.4 CLIQUE FORMATION

The result of the candidate generation process is a collection of candidates for each label in the active recognition vocabulary. Because the operators cannot be expected to be sufficiently robust, extra steps must be taken to find those candidates that truly are instances of their associated classes.

To obtain this increase in reliability, we make use of the Principle of Global Coherence (Section 2.4.2). Candidates that are not consistent with a partial image interpretation cannot be part of the final interpretation. The goal is to find a mutually consistent set of candidates that explains as much of the image as possible.

Definition 8: A *clique* is a set of mutually consistent candidate hypotheses.

Each clique represents a possible interpretation of the image. Condor builds a number of cliques and chooses the "best" one as its final interpretation. Naturally, it would be computationally infeasible to generate all possible cliques; instead, cliques are generated in a special order (described in Section 4.1.5) to increase the likelihood that a good interpretation will be found early. Thus, the longer that Condor analyzes an image, the better its interpretation is likely to be, although the chance of improving the interpretation diminishes rapidly with time.

Inconsistency is determined by special-purpose procedures whose application is mediated by Type III context rules (see also Figure 4.2).

Definition 9: Type III Context Rule – Consistency Determination:

$$L : \{CE_1, CE_2, \cdots, CE_n\} \Longrightarrow A$$

If all context elements CE_i are satisfied, then procedure A will determine if it is possible for a candidate to be an instance of class L.

Example: A candidate for **ground** cannot extend above the skyline:

GROUND :   { CLIQUE-CONTAINS(skyline) } $\Longrightarrow$

PARTIALLY-ABOVE-SKYLINE .

As was the case with candidate generation, the routines for inconsistency determination are associated with context sets that encode the assumptions necessary for their successful application. Each operator tests a candidate for consistency with all the incumbents already present in a clique. If any satisfied Type III context rule finds a candidate to be inconsistent, that candidate is not admitted into the clique, although it may participate in other cliques. Thus, consistency-determination context sets provide necessary (but not sufficient) conditions for clique inclusion.

A clique contains a collection of candidates annotated with inferred 3D properties and relations. The inconsistency operators encode geometric and physical relationships that must be consistent with known facts about the environment and the various semantic classes. The operators may involve either 2D image-plane computations or such 3D constraints as size, support, orientation, and occupancy of solid objects. The 2D constraints are useful for rapidly eliminating some candidates when they are easily seen to be inconsistent, or when sufficient 3D information cannot be established to allow more sophisticated spatial reasoning procedures to be applied. The consistency-determination context sets include context elements that specify what 3D information must be known. Their use causes an attempt to infer that information if it is not already known.

The net effect of applying Type III context rules is that consistency is checked by constructing a 3D model according to a set of conditions that prevent a nonphysically realizable situation from occurring.

4.1.5 CANDIDATE COMPARISON

The search for the largest coherent set of candidates can be combinatorially infeasible without further constraint — the number of potential cliques is exponential in the number of candidates. For this reason, cliques are generated in a special order.

At any point during the processing of an image, there will be a collection of candidates for each label to be instantiated. Some of these candidates are obviously better examples of the class denoted by the label than are others. By building cliques beginning with the best candidates of each class, we are much more likely to encounter good cliques early in the search (typically several within the first half-dozen cliques). Condor uses this best-first strategy to avoid the combinatorics that would otherwise prevent recognition.

The task here is to order the candidates within each class so the better ones may be added to cliques before the others. The difficulty is choosing a suitable metric to use for ordering. For most classes of interest in the outdoor world, no single evaluation metric gives a reliable ordering. It is possible to use multiple metrics that evaluate the candidates along various dimensions, but that would still leave the problem of comparing multidimensional evaluation vectors. To justify a weighted sum of the vector components, it would be necessary to make the unlikely assumption of some form of independence. A similar independence assumption would be required if the evaluation measures were to be given a probabilistic interpretation and combined using probability theory.

The solution we have adopted is to make use of multiple evaluators, but not to assume that they are independent in any way. Instead, they are used to compare two candidates for a given label, with each evaluator casting a vote for the candidate it ranks higher. If all evaluators favor one candidate over another, a preference ordering of the candidates is established. Otherwise, no ordering is imposed. The net effect of pairwise comparison of all candidates for a given label is to impose a partial order on those candidates. The candidates at the tops of the partial orders will be tested for consistency with the cliques before those below them.

Definition 10: An *evaluator* is a function that scores the relative likelihood that a candidate for class L is actually an instance of L.

The evaluators that apply in any context are described by candidate evaluation context sets.

Definition 11: Type II Context Rule – Candidate Evaluation:

$$L : \{CE_1, CE_2, \cdots, CE_n\} \implies A$$

If all context elements CE_i are satisfied, then A can be used as an evaluation function for comparing two candidates for the class L.

Example: When viewed obliquely, the ground should exhibit a horizontally striated texture. HORIZONTALLY-STRIATED is a function that measures this property within a candidate region:

GROUND : {CAMERA-IS-HORIZONTAL} $\implies$ HORIZONTALLY-STRIATED.

As before, the context sets allow the relevant knowledge to be subdivided into manageable pieces. The context elements encode the conditions under which a relatively simple-minded evaluation function gives meaningful information. It is intended that many evaluation functions be provided within context sets, so that robust comparisons result whenever a unanimous vote occurs.

Definition 12: Candidate C_1 is *preferred* over candidate C_2 if and only if all evaluators occurring in satisfied context sets score C_1 higher than C_2.

As always, context elements that refer to other object classes cause other computations to be triggered. Satisfied context elements also provide information for setting parameters that may be required by the associated evaluation functions.

The structure of the comparisons is noteworthy because it contrasts with the way comparisons are performed in nearly every other recognition system. The usual approach is to partition an image and to consider which of several potential class labels is the best description of a region. In Condor, we start with several partitions (candidates) and consider which of several candidates is the most likely instance of a class. For example, a conventional recognition system would consider whether a particular region was more likely to be a tree trunk or a road. Condor would have several potential delineations of a tree trunk and would consider which is the best description of the trunk.

This departs from conventional approaches in two significant ways. First, comparing candidate regions for a given label requires knowledge of the semantics of that label only, whereas the customary approach of comparing two labels for a given region requires knowledge of the relationships among many semantic categories. When considering which candidate is the best tree trunk, Condor needs to know only about tree trunks and related categories (such as branches, roots, and the ground). In contrast, deciding what label to assign to a given region using a conventional approach requires the ability to compare any pair of labels. This in turn requires knowledge of the relationships between every pair of semantic categories, a burden that grows rapidly as new classes are added to the recognition vocabulary. The Condor orientation provides a basis for believing that sufficient knowledge might eventually be encoded in the system to allow robust comparison even in a large-scale system.

Second, we enforce the condition that the comparisons lead to a preference only if one candidate is clearly a better choice than the other. With this conservative approach, we can reap additional computational savings by pruning large portions of the search for maximally consistent cliques. For example, if candidate C_1 is clearly a better instance of class L than candidate C_2 in the context of a clique K, and C_1 is found to be inconsistent with clique K, then C_2 can be eliminated as a potential member of clique K as well. Ruling out C_2 may eliminate other candidates recursively. Thus we avoid the need to test the consistency of C_2 and any of its inferiors. Furthermore, it may at times be impossible otherwise to establish C_2 as inconsistent, in which case this pruning step prevents the clique from being contaminated with a bad candidate. Although it does not follow logically that C_2 cannot be a class L instance, its elimination is a powerful heuristic that is nearly always justified. We can afford to take this chance because additional cliques will be generated simultaneously that may happen to avoid repeating an unjustified elimination. Thus even when some generators yield unreliable candidates, and the comparisons make occasional mistakes, it may still be possible to build a clique that yields a completely accurate semantic labeling of an image.

4.1.6 THE RECOGNITION PROCESS

Let us summarize the processing steps that have been described so far (Figure 4.2). For each label in the active recognition vocabulary, all Type I context sets are evaluated. The operators associated with those that are satisfied are executed, producing candidates for each class. Type II context sets that are satisfied are then used to evaluate each candidate for a class, and if all such evaluators prefer one candidate over another, a preference ordering is established between them. These preference relations are assembled to form partial orders over the candidates, one partial order for each class. Next, a search for mutually coherent sets of candidates is conducted by incrementally building cliques of consistent candidates, beginning with empty cliques. A candidate is nominated for inclusion into a clique by choosing one of the candidates at the top of one of the partial orders. Type III context sets that are satisfied are used to test the consistency of a nominee with candidates already in the clique. A consistent nominee is added to the clique; an inconsistent one is removed from further consideration with that clique. Further candidates are added to the cliques until none remain. Additional cliques are generated in a similar fashion as computational resources permit. Ultimately, one clique is selected as the best semantic labeling of the image on the basis of the portion of the image that is explained and the reliability of the operators that contributed to the clique.

Each of the processing steps occurs simultaneously in our conceptual view, but there are some implicit sequencing constraints. Candidate evaluators begin to construct partial orders as soon as candidates become available. Incremental addition of candidates to cliques begins as soon as partial orders are available. Theoretically, there is no need to wait for one stage to finish before later stages are begun, but it may be desirable when computational resources are limited.

The interaction among context sets is significant. The addition of a candidate to a clique may provide context that could trigger a previously unsatisfied context set to generate new candidates or establish new preference orderings. For example, once one bush has been recognized, it is a good idea to look specifically for similar bushes in the image. This tactic is implemented by a candidate-generation context set that includes a context element that is satisfied only when a bush is in a clique.

Similarly, as cliques evolve, the partial orders for each class may change. Ideally, all candidate generation and comparison activity should be allowed to subside before a candidate is nominated into a clique. This synchronization is an implementation issue that is not of theoretical importance because additional cliques will always be generated later.

It is important to remember that multiple cliques will be in various stages of construction simultaneously. Each clique has its own partial orders from which to choose, although many candidates will be identical in several or all of the cliques. Context-set satisfaction is determined individually for each clique.

4.2 Implementation of Condor

There are two major challenges in implementing the conceptual architecture we have described on a serial processor with finite resources.[1] One is to decide what action to perform next from among the collection of operations that could occur in parallel. This is not trivial: the result of one action could change the premises used by other actions. The second challenge is how to represent context; this issue is complicated by the need to represent and access multiple cliques without interference.

4.2.1 PROCESSING SEQUENCE

All of the computations carried out by Condor are controlled by context sets. At any given time, there might be many satisfied context sets whose operators could be invoked. Condor as implemented evaluates context sets in an order that is designed to provide additional information rapidly. For example, it is sensible to build all partial orders as completely as possible

---

[1]The architecture is intentionally well-suited for parallel processors. A serial machine was used in our experimentation strictly for convenience.

before starting to build cliques, although this is not required by the conceptual architecture. Although the context sets are evaluated in a fixed order, their satisfaction depends on the context so far derived. Thus, the order in which operators are invoked depends primarily on the contextual information. The order of context set evaluation we have chosen serves mainly to accelerate the interpretation of images.

The sequence of operations in Condor is summarized in Figure 4.3. The serialization of an inherently parallel architecture is complicated by the interdependencies among the processing steps. When first presented with an image and tasked to recognize a target vocabulary, Condor generates candidates and compares them to impose a partial order on the candidates in the target vocabulary. Any additional classes that are found to be of use are added to the active recognition vocabulary and are processed similarly. Next, a candidate from the top of one of the partial orders is added to a clique. Because this changes the context relevant to that clique, the candidate generation process is repeated and the partial orders are reevaluated in that new context. A comprehensive caching mechanism is employed to prevent reevaluating any operations that have not changed. A new nominee is chosen from the tops of the partial orders and checked for consistency with the clique. If it is found to be consistent, it is added to the clique and removed from its partial order. If inconsistent, it is removed from further consideration for membership in that clique, although it may join another clique later. The inconsistent nominee is removed from its partial order along with any candidate over which it is preferred. This cycle is repeated until no candidates remain for nomination, thus completing the development of the first clique.

Additional cliques are generated by iterating the entire process. Any operations that occurred before construction of the first clique began need not be repeated as their context is still valid. Unnecessary repetition is avoided by rewinding to the beginning of clique construction before starting to build the second clique. Condor generates additional cliques by nominating candidates in different sequences. Many strategies exist for selecting candidate sequences and the heuristic nominating function can be modified to implement them. The strategy that Condor routinely uses is to seed each clique with a candidate that had been ruled out by an earlier clique, thereby guaranteeing that a new and different clique will result.

After each clique is completed, it is compared with the best previous

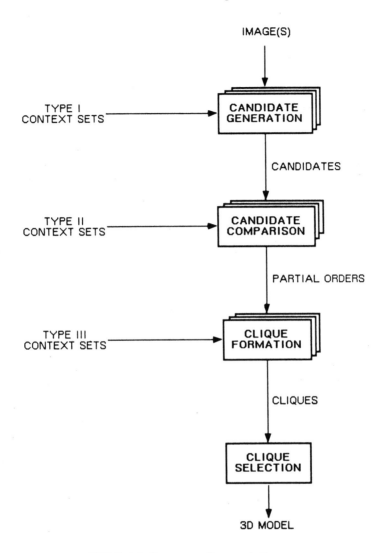

FIGURE 4.3. Sequence of computation.

clique to determine which interpretation of the image is better. There is no theoretically sound way of comparing two cliques, and the method we employ is somewhat *ad hoc*. Each clique is scored on the basis of the portion of the image that is explained, the specificity of each label, and the reliability of the operators that generated the candidates in the clique. The higher scoring clique is retained and additional cliques are generated until a scoring threshold is exceeded or available computation time is exhausted. At that point, the highest scoring clique is accepted as the best interpretation of the image, and the candidates it contains are considered to have been recognized.

The contents of this best clique are then used to update the 3D model of the environment. Newly found objects are inserted in the Core Knowledge Structure. Candidates depicting previously known objects are used to update the location, size, shape, and appearance of that object in the CKS. The name of the operator that successfully delineated each object in the image is stored with the object so that it might be invoked again when that object next comes in the field of view. The result is an updated model of the visual world, which will provide more context for the recognition of objects in subsequent images.

4.2.2   REPRESENTATION OF CONTEXT

Because Condor has been designed to make use of a persistent store of information about the visual world, it is necessary to provide a mechanism for its representation. Condor requires access to scene objects based on their location and various semantic properties. The Core Knowledge Structure (CKS) provides this necessary access.

The CKS is an object-oriented knowledge/database that was specifically designed to serve as the central information manager for a perceptual system such as an autonomous outdoor robot [Smith and Strat 1987, Strat and Smith 1988b]. Four facilities of the CKS are of particular importance for Condor (see Appendix A for further detail):

Multiple resolution — The CKS employs a multiresolution octree to locate objects only as precisely as warranted by the data. Similarly, a collection of geometric modeling primitives are available to represent objects at an appropriate level of detail. In parallel with the octree for spatial resolution is a semantic network that represents things at multiple levels of semantic resolution. Condor's recognition vocabulary is represented as nodes in the semantic network, which allows the system to refer to objects at an appropriate level in the abstraction hierarchy.

Inheritance and inference — The CKS uses the semantic network to perform some limited types of inference when querying the data store. Thus, query responses are assembled not only from those objects that syntactically match the query, but also from objects that can be inferred to match given the relations encoded in the semantic network. For example, the CKS can be queried for all trees within ten meters of any dirt road, and will find all such trees regardless of whether they were originally categorized as oaks or pines or whether any roadway was present when they were instantiated in the database. Spatial inference is provided based on geometric constraints computed by the octree manipulation routines. Inheritance of attributes that are unspecified is performed in a similar fashion. For example, a query for all objects taller than five meters will be satisfied by all trees not specifically known to be shorter than five meters, but not satisfied by any rocks (unless they are individually known to be higher than five meters).

Accommodation of conflicting data — One of the realities of analyzing imagery of the real world is that conflicts will result from mistakes in interpretation and from unnoticed changes in the world. The database used by Condor must not collapse when conflicting information is stored. Because the CKS treats all incoming data as the opinions of the data sources, logical inconsistencies will not corrupt the database. Similarly, values derived through multiple inheritance paths are treated as multiple opinions. This strategy has several advantages and disadvantages. Rather than fusing information as it arises, the CKS has the option of postponing combination until its results are needed. This means that the fusion can be performed on the basis of additional information that may become available, and in a manner that depends on the immediate task at hand. Some information may never be needed, in which case the CKS may forgo its combination entirely. The disadvantages are a need to store a larger quantity of data and a slowed response at retrieval time.

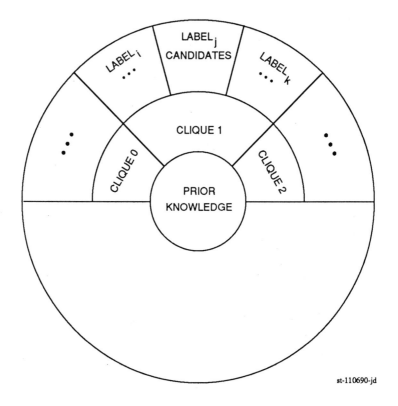

FIGURE 4.4. Partition of information within CKS.

For an object recognition system such as Condor, the CKS seems to provide the right tradeoff. Condor uses the multiple opinion facility to store the attributes of recognized objects. Each attribute value is annotated with the image in which it was identified, its time of acquisition, and its time of recognition. In so doing, it is possible to reason about the validity of the stored data, and to react accordingly.

The opinion mechanism is also used to store multiple cliques in Condor. Each candidate is stored in the CKS as the opinion of the clique to which it pertains. This partition of information is shown schematically in Figure 4.4. Each sector of the "pie" contains the opinions of one clique. Contextual information is ascertained by accessing data within the clique's sector or in the central core, which represents data shared by all cliques. For example, prior information and recognition results from previous images are in the central core, available to all cliques.

User interface — Although Condor is designed to be a fully automated recognition system, a comprehensive user interface is invaluable for development and debugging. The CKS provides a menu-driven query mechanism that is useful for inspecting the intermediate states of computation. In addition, the CKS has been integrated with SRI's Cartographic Modeling Environment [Hanson and Quam 1988] to provide a capability of generating synthetic views of terrain. This allows one to visualize the contents of the database from an arbitrary viewpoint by rendering a synthetic image. Doing so provides a window into the information that Condor is assuming as it interprets an image.

4.2.3 CONTEXT-SET CONSTRUCTION

Context sets are the key to any recognition abilities that Condor demonstrates. While we cannot offer a prescription for designing context sets, we can provide some insight based on our experience in building context sets for natural-object recognition.

Type I context rules (candidate generation) are constructed based on an assessment of what operators may work for each label in the recognition vocabulary. Using a representative sample of imagery from the target domain, we composed image-processing operations that work reasonably well in various circumstances. Factors that influenced the choice of which operators to include were: likelihood of success, ease of implementation, the lack of any alternative operators, and the availability of existing code. Distinct operators are provided to generate hypotheses for natural objects when viewed from qualitatively different perspectives or resolution. Table 4.1 lists the types of operators that are actually employed by Condor to generate candidates for the Stanford foothill experimentation site. For each operator, the assumptions that it requires are encoded as context elements in a context set that controls the invocation of the operator. These context elements limit the situations in which the operator will be applied, ensure the existence of any required data, and establish the parameter settings associated with the operator.

Algorithm	Explanation
Association	Finds connected sets of pixels in a binary image.
Striations	Finds the orientation and strength of local texture.
Delineation	Finds line-like structure.
Outlining	Finds the boundary of a region.
Thresholding	Uses scale-space techniques to choose thresholds.
Edge-finders	Any of several well-known edge-finding routines
Contrast enhancement	Stretches the histogram of an image.
Smoothing	Low-pass filter
Histogramming	Computes a histogram and associated statistics.
Snakes	Optimizes a deformable model to find the best fit.
Texture	Any of several well-known algorithms for measuring texture
Segmentation	Completely partitions an image using KNIFE [Laws 1988].
Dense stereo	Computes a dense depth image using CYCLOPS [Barnard 1989].
Sparse stereo	Computes depths at some easily correlated points [Hannah 1985].
Homogeneity	A noise tolerant algorithm for measuring local homogeneity

TABLE 4.1. Categories of candidate-generation operators.

Type II context rules (candidate evaluation) are assembled from evaluation metrics that can be used to compare two candidates. Context elements that define the conditions under which the metrics are meaningful are collected into context sets for each label in the recognition vocabulary. The metrics themselves need not order candidates perfectly, but should perform substantially better than a random ordering. Because Condor requires a unanimous vote of all applicable metrics before ordering two candidates, the inclusion of a faulty metric may cause some candidates to remain unordered, but will not cause any to be reverse ordered. It is important that preferences be correct when they are made. Flat orderings require more cliques to be searched but do not lead to incorrect recognition results, whereas incorrect orderings may cause valid interpretations to be missed. Table 4.2 shows some of the evaluation metrics that Condor uses.

Type III context rules define the conditions under which inconsistency of a candidate with the other members of a clique can be established. To form Type III context rules, we encode and assemble constraints that make it impossible for a candidate hypothesis to be valid given the assumption that the candidates already in the clique are correct. It is important that inconsistent candidates be correctly identified so that physically impossible cliques are not constructed. However, it is not necessary that a complete definition of consistent candidates be encoded. This asymmetry was designed intentionally because it is far simpler to specify what could not be a tree, for example, than it is to specify what is a tree. Some of the consistency-determination constraints used by Condor are listed in Table 4.3.

4.3   Example of natural-object recognition

To illustrate the basic processing sequence, Condor was tasked to recognize the sky, the ground, and the foliage appearing in the image shown in Figure 2.3. This relatively easy image was acquired in the foothills portion of the Stanford University campus in the afternoon of a sunny day using an ordinary 35mm camera. To make the description as clear as possible, some of the machinery incorporated in Condor has been deactivated while creating this example. In particular, no prior knowledge of the topography or features on the terrain is used. The digitized image is a single monochrome 8-bit frame; no color, stereo, or other range data are used.

TABLE 4.2. Evaluation metrics.

Evaluation metric	Explanation
ABOVE-HORIZON	Raised objects are more likely found above the horizon.
ABOVE-SKYLINE	Raised objects above the skyline are preferred.
BELOW-HORIZON	Prefer ground candidates below the horizon.
BELOW-SKYLINE	Prefer ground candidates below the skyline.
BLUE	Prefer blue sky candidates on a sunny day.
BRIGHT	Prefer bright sky candidates.
ELLIPSOIDAL	Prefer ellipsoidal bushes and tree-crowns (in 3D).
ELLIPTIC	Prefer bushes that are shaped like ellipses (in 2D).
GREEN	Prefer green grass in the winter and spring in California.
HIGHLY-TEXTURED	Prefer foliage candidates that are highly textured.
HORIZONTAL	Prefer ground candidates that are horizontal (in 3D).
HORIZONTALLY-STRIATED	Prefer ground candidates that exhibit horizontal striations.
NEAR-TOP	Prefer sky candidates that are near the top of the image.
NO-SKY-BELOW	Prefer bush and rock candidates that are not above the sky.
REASONABLE-SIZE	Prefer trees and bushes that are sized appropriately.
SIMILAR-COLOR	Prefer candidates that are similar in color to known objects.
SIMILAR-TEXTURE	Prefer candidates that have similar texture as a known object.
UNDEFINED-RANGE	Prefer sky candidates that are uncorrelated in stereo.
2D-VERTICALITY	Prefer tree trunks that are approximately vertical in the image.
3D-VERTICALITY	When range is available, prefer tree trunks that are vertical.

TABLE 4.3. Consistency constraints.

Consistency constraint	Explanation
ABOVE-SKY-REGION	Most objects must not be completely off the ground.
LEANING	Objects that lean too much are unsupported.
MISMATCHED-BRIGHTNESS	The intensity of sky must vary smoothly.
NOT-SUPPORTED-BY-GROUND	Most plants must be rooted in the ground.
OVERLAPS-IN-IMAGE	Inconsistent labels are prohibited.
PARTIALLY-ABOVE-SKYLINE	The ground cannot extend above the skyline.
PARTIALLY-BELOW-HORIZON	The sky cannot extend below the horizon.

4.3.1 CANDIDATE GENERATION

Condor begins by generating candidates for each of the classes in the target vocabulary. The relevant candidate generation context sets are shown in Table 4.4. Tables 4.5 and 4.6 show the relevant Type II and Type III context sets used in this example. During the generation of candidates for the sky label, Context Set 5 was not satisfied because no color image is available and Context Set 6 was not satisfied because no candidates have been selected yet for inclusion in a clique. Context Sets 1 through 4 are satisfied and the sky candidates they generate are shown in Figure 4.5(a).

The operator WEAKLY-STRIATED-REGIONS happened to generate no candidates, even though its context set was satisfied. The SEGMENTATION-REGIONS operator returns the regions found by a conventional segmentation algorithm (Candidates 909, 910, and 911). A fourth region, corresponding to the lower third of the image, was also generated, but immediately rejected by an application of the Type III consistency-determination context rules, which eliminate candidates that are unacceptable in any clique. In this case, for consistency determination, Context Sets 81 through 84 were tested for satisfaction. A side result of testing Context Set 81 was to add geometric-horizon to the active recognition vocabulary. Because the geometric horizon for this image was given, Context Set 81 is satisfied and its operator, PARTIALLY-BELOW-GEOMETRIC-HORIZON, eliminates the fourth segmentation region because it is below the geometric horizon and, therefore, could never be sky.

Notice that three of the candidates (910, 912, and 914) are fairly similar — Condor must eventually sort out which to include in each clique, based on how well they fit in the context of other members in the clique.

Ground candidates are generated by Context Sets 7 through 10 and are shown in Figure 4.5(b). Context Set 7 is satisfied and yields the same four regions obtained using the conventional segmentation operation. Context Set 8 is also satisfied and is used to extract the horizontally striated region depicted as Candidate 919. Because of foreshortening, horizontal surfaces tend to appear to have horizontal striations when viewed obliquely. This explains why CAMERA-IS-HORIZONTAL is included as a context element essential for invoking the HORIZONTAL-STRIATIONS operator to find ground candidates. In this case, most of the ground exhibits horizontal texture, but some of the foliage was horizontally striated as well and is merged with this candidate. Context Sets 9 and 10 are not satisfied.

#	Class	Context elements	Operator
1	SKY	CLIQUE-IS-EMPTY	SEGMENTATION-REGIONS
2	SKY	CLIQUE-IS-EMPTY	WEAKLY-TEXTURED-REGIONS
3	SKY	CLIQUE-IS-EMPTY	WEAKLY-STRIATED-REGIONS
4	SKY	CLIQUE-IS-EMPTY	BRIGHT-REGIONS
5	SKY	CLIQUE-IS-EMPTY ∧ SKY-IS-CLEAR ∧ RGB-IS-AVAILABLE	BLUE-REGIONS
6	SKY	LAST-CANDIDATE-IS(sky)	SIMILAR-REGIONS
7	GROUND	CLIQUE-IS-EMPTY	SEGMENTATION-REGIONS
8	GROUND	CLIQUE-IS-EMPTY ∧ CAMERA-IS-HORIZONTAL	HORIZONTAL-STRIATION-REGIONS
9	GROUND	CLIQUE-IS-EMPTY ∧ DENSE-RANGE-IS-AVAILABLE	HORIZONTAL-SURFACE-PATCHES
10	GROUND	LAST-CANDIDATE-IS(ground)	SIMILAR-REGIONS-REGIONS
11	FOLIAGE	CLIQUE-IS-EMPTY	TEXTURE-ABOVE-THRESHOLD
12	FOLIAGE	CLIQUE-IS-EMPTY	VEGETATIVE-TRANSPARENCY
13	FOLIAGE	CLIQUE-IS-EMPTY ∧ RGB-IS-AVAILABLE	GREEN-REGIONS
14	FOLIAGE	LAST-CANDIDATE-IS(foliage)	SIMILAR-REGIONS
15	FOLIAGE	CLIQUE-IS-EMPTY ∧ DENSE-RANGE-IS-AVAILABLE	HIGHLY-FRACTAL-REGIONS
16	RAISED-OBJECT	CLIQUE-IS-EMPTY	SEGMENTATION-REGIONS
17	RAISED-OBJECT	CLIQUE-IS-EMPTY	VERTICAL-STRIATION-REGIONS
18	RAISED-OBJECT	CLIQUE-IS-EMPTY ∧ DENSE-RANGE-IS-AVAILABLE	DENSE-REGIONS-ABOVE-GROUND
19	RAISED-OBJECT	CLIQUE-IS-EMPTY ∧ SPARSE-RANGE-IS-AVAILABLE	SPARSE-REGIONS-ABOVE-GROUND
20	RAISED-OBJECT	LAST-CANDIDATE-IS(complete-sky)	NON-SKY-REGIONS-ABOVE-SKYLINE
21	COMPLETE-GROUND	LAST-CANDIDATE-IS(geometric-horizon)	REGION-BELOW-GEOMETRIC-HORIZON
22	COMPLETE-GROUND	LAST-CANDIDATE-IS(ground)	UNION-OF-GROUND-REGIONS
23	COMPLETE-GROUND	LAST-CANDIDATE-IS(skyline)	REGION-BELOW-SKYLINE
25	COMPLETE-SKY	LAST-CANDIDATE-IS(sky) ∧ SITE-IS(Stanford-hills)	UNION-OF-SKY-REGIONS

TABLE 4.4. Type I Context Sets: Candidate Generation.

#	Class	Context elements	Operator
41	SKY	ALWAYS	ABOVE-GEOMETRIC-HORIZON
42	SKY	SKY-IS-CLEAR ∧ TIME-IS-DAY	BRIGHT
43	SKY	SKY-IS-CLEAR ∧ TIME-IS-DAY	UNTEXTURED
44	SKY	SKY-IS-CLEAR ∧ TIME-IS-DAY ∧ RGB-IS-AVAILABLE	BLUE
45	SKY	SKY-IS-OVERCAST ∧ TIME-IS-DAY	BRIGHT
46	SKY	SKY-IS-OVERCAST ∧ TIME-IS-DAY	UNTEXTURED
47	SKY	SKY-IS-OVERCAST ∧ TIME-IS-DAY ∧ RGB-IS-AVAILABLE	WHITE
48	SKY	SPARSE-RANGE-IS-AVAILABLE	SPARSE-RANGE-IS-UNDEFINED
49	SKY	CAMERA-IS-HORIZONTAL	NEAR-TOP
50	SKY	CAMERA-IS-HORIZONTAL ∧ CLIQUE-CONTAINS(complete-sky)	ABOVE-SKYLINE
51	SKY	CLIQUE-CONTAINS(sky)	SIMILAR-INTENSITY
52	SKY	CLIQUE-CONTAINS(sky)	SIMILAR-TEXTURE
53	SKY	RGB-IS-AVAILABLE ∧ CLIQUE-CONTAINS(sky)	SIMILAR-COLOR
61	GROUND	CAMERA-IS-HORIZONTAL	HORIZONTALLY-STRIATED
62	GROUND	CAMERA-IS-HORIZONTAL	NEAR-BOTTOM
63	GROUND	SPARSE-RANGE-IS-AVAILABLE	SPARSE-RANGES-ARE-HORIZONTAL
64	GROUND	DENSE-RANGE-IS-AVAILABLE	DENSE-RANGES-ARE-HORIZONTAL
65	GROUND	CAMERA-IS-HORIZONTAL ∧ CLIQUE-CONTAINS(complete-ground)	BELOW-SKYLINE
66	GROUND	CAMERA-IS-HORIZONTAL ∧ CLIQUE-CONTAINS(geometric-horizon) ∧ ¬ CLIQUE-CONTAINS(skyline)	BELOW-GEOMETRIC-HORIZON
67	GROUND	TIME-IS-DAY	DARK
71	FOLIAGE	ALWAYS	HIGHLY-TEXTURED
72	FOLIAGE	ALWAYS	VEGETATIVE-TRANSPARENCY
73	FOLIAGE	CAMERA-IS-HORIZONTAL	NEAR-TOP
74	FOLIAGE	RGB-IS-AVAILABLE	GREEN
76	RAISED-OBJECT	SPARSE-RANGE-IS-AVAILABLE	SPARSE-HEIGHT-ABOVE-GROUND
77	RAISED-OBJECT	DENSE-RANGE-IS-AVAILABLE	DENSE-HEIGHT-ABOVE-GROUND
78	RAISED-OBJECT	CAMERA-IS-HORIZONTAL ∧ CLIQUE-CONTAINS(complete-sky)	ABOVE-SKYLINE

TABLE 4.5. Type II Context Sets: Candidate Evaluation.

909 SEGMENTATION-REGIONS

915 SEGMENTATION-REGIONS

920 VEGETATIVE-TRANSPARENCY

910 SEGMENTATION-REGIONS

916 SEGMENTATION-REGIONS

921 VEGETATIVE-TRANSPARENCY

911 SEGMENTATION-REGIONS

917 SEGMENTATION-REGIONS

922 TEXTURE-ABOVE-THRESHOLD

912 WEAKLY-TEXTURED-REGIONS

918 SEGMENTATION-REGIONS

923 TEXTURE-ABOVE-THRESHOLD

914 BRIGHT-REGIONS

919 HORIZONTAL-STRIATION-REGIONS

924 SEGMENTATION-REGIONS

925 SEGMENTATION-REGIONS

926 SEGMENTATION-REGIONS

927 SEGMENTATION-REGIONS

928 VERTICAL-STRIATION-REGIONS

(a) sky   (b) ground   (c) foilage

FIGURE 4.5. Some candidates generated by Condor.

#	Class	Context elements	Operator
81	SKY	GEOMETRIC-HORIZON-KNOWN	PARTIALLY-BELOW-GEOMETRIC-HORIZON
82	SKY	ADDING-TO-CLIQUE	INCONSISTENT-WITH-CLIQUE
83	SKY	ADDING-TO-CLIQUE ∧ CLIQUE-CONTAINS(sky)	MISMATCHED-BRIGHTNESS
84	SKY	SPARSE-RANGE-IS-AVAILABLE	MUST-NOT-HAVE-FINITE-RANGE
87	GROUND	CLIQUE-CONTAINS(complete-sky)	PARTIALLY-ABOVE-SKYLINE
88	GROUND	ADDING-TO-CLIQUE	INCONSISTENT-WITH-CLIQUE
89	GROUND	DENSE-RANGE-IS-AVAILABLE	SLOPE-TOO-STEEP
91	FOLIAGE	ADDING-TO-CLIQUE	INCONSISTENT-WITH-CLIQUE
93	COMPLETE-GROUND	ADDING-TO-CLIQUE	INCONSISTENT-WITH-CLIQUE

TABLE 4.6. Type III Context Sets: Consistency Determination.

Foliage candidates are generated by Context Sets 11 through 15. In addition, the candidate generation context sets for **raised-object** are used to generate **foliage** candidates as well because **foliage** is a subcategory of **raised-object** in the abstraction hierarchy (Figure 3.1). Therefore, any **raised-object** candidates are also candidates for **foliage**. Condor always employs context sets for all superclasses — the CKS returns them automatically when queried by Condor. The **foliage** candidates are depicted in Figure 4.5(c).

4.3.2 CANDIDATE COMPARISON

Next, Condor compares the candidates for each class to construct the partial orders. Candidate-Evaluation Context Rules 41 through 53 are used for evaluating **sky** candidates. Only Context Sets 41, 42, 43, and 49 are satisfied. Their associated operators are used to evaluate each of the **sky** candidates and the result is tabulated below. Each evaluator returns a score between 0.0 and 1.0. Only the relative magnitude of this score for each evaluator is meaningful. The scores are not normalized across evaluators because there is no basis for doing so.

Examining Table 4.7 reveals that every evaluator scored Candidate 910 as high as or higher than Candidate 909. Therefore, 910 is preferred over 909 as a **sky** candidate. Other unanimous preferences are

$$910 \succ 914, \quad 912 \succ 909, \quad 912 \succ 914, \quad \text{and} \quad 914 \succ 909 \,.$$

TABLE 4.7. Initial evaluation of sky candidates.

	Candidate				
Evaluator	909	910	911	912	914
ABOVE-GEOMETRIC-HORIZON	1.00	1.00	1.00	1.00	1.00
BRIGHT	0.44	0.71	0.94	0.76	0.67
UNTEXTURED	0.19	0.67	0.52	0.50	0.36
NEAR-TOP	0.51	0.79	0.37	0.73	0.66

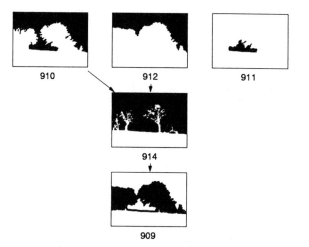

FIGURE 4.6. Partial order of candidates for sky.

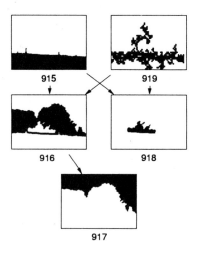

FIGURE 4.7. Partial order of candidates for ground.

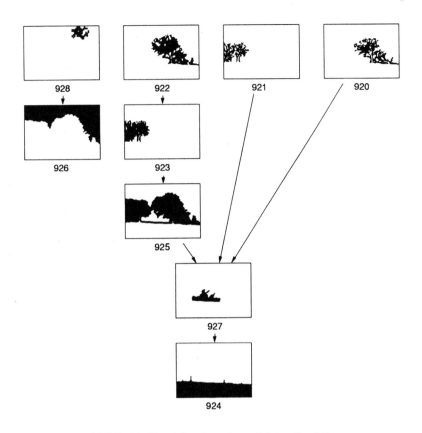

FIGURE 4.8. Partial order of candidates for foliage.

These relations are assembled into a partial order and displayed in Figure 4.6, after removing transitivities. Candidate 909, which roughly delineates the trees, is at the bottom of the partial order, as one would hope. Candidates 910, 911, and 912 were found to be equally promising sky regions. Context Set 50 would have been satisfied if a complete-sky candidate was already in the clique. There is none, but Condor adds complete-sky to the active recognition vocabulary.

Invocation of candidate evaluation context rules for ground candidates identifies three relevant evaluators, HORIZONTALLY-STRIATED, NEAR-BOTTOM, and DARK, from Context Rules 61, 62, and 67. Their results are tabulated in Table 4.8 and displayed as a partial order in Figure 4.7. Candidate 915 is the only one that can correctly be called ground, and it is indeed at the top of the partial order. Evaluation of Context Sets 65 and 66 causes complete-ground and skyline to be added to the recognition vocabulary.

TABLE 4.8. Initial evaluation of ground candidates.

	Candidate				
Evaluator	915	916	917	918	919
HORIZONTALLY-STRIATED	0.45	0.11	0.11	0.11	0.55
NEAR-BOTTOM	0.87	0.49	0.21	0.63	0.71
DARK	0.82	0.56	0.29	0.06	0.64

Comparison of foliage candidates results in the partial order shown in Figure 4.8. Type II context sets for foliage yield three relevant evaluators (Table 4.9). The Type II context sets for raised-object are also tested to identify additional evaluators, but none are satisfied.

TABLE 4.9. Initial evaluation of foliage candidates.

	Candidate								
Evaluator	920	921	922	923	924	925	926	927	928
HIGHLY-TEXTURED	0.93	0.91	0.87	0.86	0.41	0.81	0.33	0.48	0.35
VEGETATIVE-TRANSPARENCY	0.93	0.92	0.88	0.87	0.45	0.85	0.45	0.52	0.45
NEAR-TOP	0.48	0.49	0.53	0.52	0.13	0.51	0.79	0.37	0.88

The active recognition vocabulary is now {sky, ground, foliage, geometric-horizon, complete-sky, complete-ground, and skyline} and Condor proceeds to generate candidates and partial orders for the balance of these classes.[2]

4.3.3 CLIQUE FORMATION

At this point, all satisfied context sets for classes in the active recognition vocabulary have been employed and Condor begins to build cliques of mutually consistent candidates. The candidates at the tops of the four partial orders are eligible to be introduced into an (empty) clique. The choice of which candidate to nominate first is made with the aid of a heuristic that chooses on the basis of the reliability of the operator that generated the candidate, the desirability of adding the candidate's class to the clique, the nearness of the candidate to the camera, and the size of the candidate. If this choice is made poorly, it may lead to a small clique and more cliques will have to be generated before a large, mutually coherent clique is constructed. Figure 4.9 shows the order in which candidates were actually nominated for inclusion in the first clique.

According to the heuristic, the **geometric-horizon** candidate is chosen first and added as the sole candidate in Clique 1. This tentative conclusion constitutes new context, albeit for Clique 1 only. All Type I context sets are reevaluated to see if any new candidates are generated, and all Type II context sets are reevaluated to update the partial orders. The only new candidate that is produced is a **complete-ground** candidate generated by Context Set 21. Type II Context Set 66 is now satisfied and adds BELOW-GEOMETRIC-HORIZON to the list of evaluators for ground candidates. Its use happens to cause no changes in the **ground** partial order.

The second candidate nominated for inclusion in the clique is the **complete-ground** candidate just generated. It is found to be consistent with the clique and is added to it. Reevaluation of all context sets provides no significant changes.

At this point, there are three candidates at the top of the **sky** partial order (Candidates 910, 911, and 912); there are two top **ground** candidates (915 and 919); and there are four top **foliage** candidates (920, 921, 922, and 928). The heuristic selection function chooses **sky** Candidate 912 to be tested for consistency with Clique 1. It is found to be consistent, is added to the clique, and all context sets are reevaluated. This time, Context Set 25 is satisfied,

---

[2]These are of no special interest and are not shown.

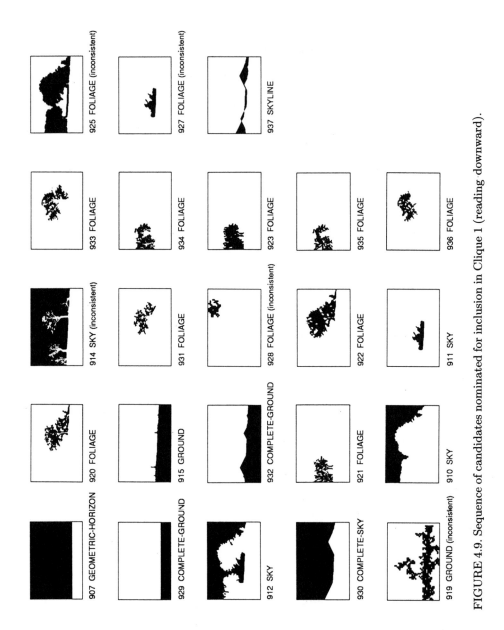

FIGURE 4.9. Sequence of candidates nominated for inclusion in Clique 1 (reading downward).

and a candidate for complete-sky is generated by the operator UNION-OF-SKY-REGIONS, which grows the existing sky region using the constraint that the ground does not slope more than 30 degrees in this area. Context Set 6 is also satisfied, and it employs the SIMILAR-REGIONS operator to find additional sky candidates that are similar to Candidate 912 in texture and intensity using an adaptive threshold algorithm. This implements the idea that anything similar in appearance to a region that is known to be sky is likely to be sky itself. Later comparison with other candidates and checking for consistency with cliques will determine if this is in fact correct. Type II Context Sets 51 and 52 are now satisfied and yield two new evaluators for comparing sky candidates. The new evaluation table is shown as Table 4.10.

TABLE 4.10. Reevaluation of sky candidates.

	Candidate			
Evaluator	909	910	911	914
ABOVE-GEOMETRIC-HORIZON	1.00	1.00	1.00	1.00
BRIGHT	0.44	0.71	0.94	0.67
UNTEXTURED	0.19	0.67	0.52	0.36
NEAR-TOP	0.51	0.79	0.37	0.66
SIMILAR-INTENSITY	0.72	0.96	0.76	0.95
SIMILAR-TEXTURE	0.42	0.94	0.94	0.81

From this table it is computed that

$$910 \succ 909, \quad 910 \succ 914, \quad \text{and} \quad 914 \succ 909$$

and the sky partial order is updated.

The newly created complete-sky candidate is the next one added to the clique. After reevaluating context sets, ground candidate 919 is nominated for inclusion next. Type III Context Rules 87 through 89 are used to test the consistency of Candidate 919 with the clique. Context Set 87 is satisfied and execution of its operation PARTIALLY-ABOVE-SKYLINE finds that ground Candidate 919 extends above the skyline and is therefore inconsistent with this clique. It is eliminated from further consideration, along with Candidates 916, 917, and 918, which are pruned from the ground partial order. This leaves Candidate 915 as the only remaining ground candidate.

Condor next nominates foliage Candidate 920, which is found to be consistent, and ground Candidate 915, which is also found to be consistent.

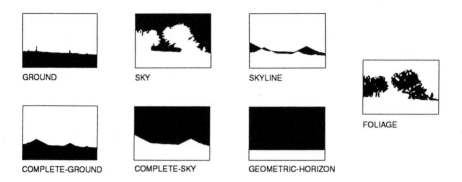

FIGURE 4.10. Composite labeling found by Clique 1.

Condor continues its processing in this manner, until no candidates remain to be tested. Figure 4.9 shows the complete sequence of nominations to the first clique. The composite labeling of the image that results from those that were accepted is given by Figure 4.10. A total of 36 candidates were generated for this clique, 50% of which were accepted in the clique while 22% were pruned without testing.

4.3.4 CLIQUE SELECTION

In this case, the first clique generated did a good job recognizing the target vocabulary, but Condor has no definitive way of knowing this. Condor generates additional cliques to see if its interpretation can be improved. The sequence of candidates nominated for inclusion in Clique 2 is shown in Figure 4.11. This clique starts with sky Candidate 914, which was ruled out by Clique 1 as being too aggressive in finding the boundary of the sky. By assuming that Candidate 914 is indeed a good delineation of sky, Clique 2 later rules out the foliage candidates (see Figure 4.11). As a result, nothing explains the foliated area very well, and Candidate 909 is eventually accepted as being sky, thereby mislabeling the entire top two-thirds of the image as sky. The composite labeling found by Clique 2 is given in Figure 4.12. A total of 32 candidates were generated for Clique 2, of which 34% were admitted and 25% were pruned.

A third clique was also generated by Condor. This one started by including the ground candidate (919) that was generated by the HORIZONTAL-STRIATIONS operator and included part of the foliage in the ground region.

914 SKY   921 FOLIAGE (inconsistent)   923 FOLIAGE (inconsistent)   909 SKY

907 GEOMETRIC-HORIZON   928 FOLIAGE (inconsistent)   927 FOLIAGE (inconsistent)   941 COMPLETE-SKY

938 COMPLETE-GROUND   915 GROUND   912 SKY   911 SKY (inconsistent)

919 GROUND (inconsistent)   939 COMPLETE-GROUND   940 COMPLETE-SKY   942 SKYLINE

920 FOLIAGE (inconsistent)   922 FOLIAGE (inconsistent)   910 SKY

FIGURE 4.11. Sequence of candidates nominated for inclusion in Clique 2.

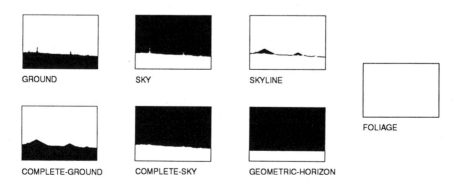

GROUND   SKY   SKYLINE   FOLIAGE

COMPLETE-GROUND   COMPLETE-SKY   GEOMETRIC-HORIZON

FIGURE 4.12. Composite labeling found by Clique 2.

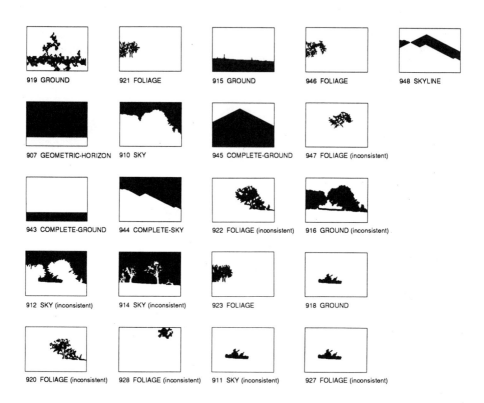

FIGURE 4.13. Sequence of candidates nominated for inclusion in Clique 3.

Its inclusion results in some of the sky being labeled as **ground** and some of the foliage being left unlabeled. Clique 3 is depicted by Figures 4.13 and 4.14. Of 33 regions generated, 36% were admitted and 21% were pruned.

Additional cliques could be generated by Condor in hopes of improving the interpretation. Among the first three, Clique 1 is selected by Condor as being the best recognition result because it explains more of the image than does Clique 3, and the composite reliability of the admitted candidates is higher than that of both Clique 2 and Clique 3.

At this point, Condor normally stores its recognition results in the CKS database to be used as context for future reference. In this example, however, Condor did not attempt to extract 3D constraints that would be useful for sizing and positioning the foliage objects it found. In Chapter 5, several examples are presented that demonstrate the capability to recover 3D geometry and to update the 3D models maintained by the CKS.

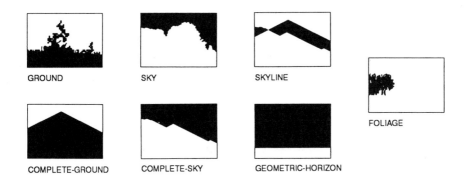

GROUND   SKY   SKYLINE   FOLIAGE

COMPLETE-GROUND   COMPLETE-SKY   GEOMETRIC-HORIZON

FIGURE 4.14. Composite labeling found by Clique 3.

4.4   Automated knowledge acquisition

The quality of Condor's recognition ability is directly tied to the quality of the context rules in its knowledge base. It is unreasonable to expect that a knowledge base of a scope sufficient to enable realistic application can be constructed entirely by hand. Therefore, like any knowledge-based vision system, Condor must have the ability to acquire knowledge automatically through experience in performing its intended task.

Although the field of machine learning has progressed rapidly in the last five years, there does not yet exist a theory of sufficient utility for use in a visual recognition system such as Condor. While the focus of our research has not been to advance the state of the art in machine learning, we recognize the importance of automated knowledge acquisition to machine vision and have made provisions in the Condor architecture to enable some forms of learning.

The Condor architecture is well-suited to the automation of knowledge acquisition for the following reasons:

- Context rules, and the context sets embedded within them, are a declarative representation that can be examined and modified by a learning algorithm.

- Condor uses its own results. Rather than analyzing each new image from scratch, Condor stores its recognition results in a persistent database. This database establishes context, which Condor exploits to analyze subsequent images. In this way, the more objects Condor has recognized, the more it is able to recognize.

- Condor is not reliant on any single part of the system being 100% correct. Indeed, nearly every aspect of the architecture was included to achieve robust recognition results in the presence of unreliable procedures and inconsistent data. This approach has beneficial implications to a learning algorithm in a vision system, which must necessarily cope with occasionally incorrect and ambiguous data. Some incorrect generalizations made by an embedded learning component will not corrupt the integrity of the overall system.

Image-understanding systems also pose some impediments to attempts to endow them with automated learning algorithms:

- The image data presented to a recognition system constitute a noisy environment for which there are few clear-cut cases, particularly in the outdoor world. Any training examples constructed will rely on subjective judgments and will contain inconsistencies. The literature on automated learning from noisy examples is sparse, and is limited mainly to statistical estimation.

- Ideally, a learning algorithm will have access to a large number of examples from which to generalize. In our experimentation we have been limited to images acquired and digitized individually, and have used only about 40 images. This limitation is compounded by the fact that analysis of a single image can require up to 20 minutes per clique, and by the desire to recognize coarse-grained objects, such as trails and trees. Thus each image yields only a few examples of each concept and thousands of images would be required to fuel a learning algorithm.[3]

It is important to discriminate among the many forms of learning. Within the Condor framework, four types of learning are of primary interest:

- Learning a description of the environment

---

[3]The use of new video frame-grabbers on a robotic platform and the use of pixel-parallel processors could enable Condor to process thousands of images in seconds per frame.

- Applying recognition procedures more effectively

- Refining context sets

- Discovering new procedures

We discuss each of these learning opportunities below.

4.4.1 LEARNING A DESCRIPTION OF THE ENVIRONMENT

In our scenario, Condor is mounted on an autonomous vehicle and tasked with identifying significant features in the immediate vicinity. Starting with an empty database, Condor adds its recognition results to the CKS after analyzing each image. After some period of time, the database contains a detailed description of all recognized features in the environment. Experiment 2 (described in Chapter 5) illustrates Condor's ability to learn a description of its surroundings. Several issues arise in the construction of 3D models and in updating a persistent world model.

When Condor has recognized an object, such as a tree, it must determine the 3D location of that object in order to store it in the world model. Condor has several facilities for accomplishing this:

- When range data are available through stereopsis or a laser rangefinder, the distance to the tree is immediately available. Together with approximate knowledge of the camera's location and orientation, the world position of the tree can be bounded. The tree is stored in the CKS within this volume using the multiresolution facilities of the CKS spatial directory.

- When no range data are available, Condor uses a digital terrain model (DTM) to estimate the location. Intersecting the DTM with the ray in space that passes from the center of projection through the base of the tree trunk in the image (which is presumed to be on the ground) allows an estimate of the tree's location to be obtained. The volume of uncertainty inherent in this procedure is stored in the CKS as the possible location of the tree.

- Without range data or a DTM, Condor can still estimate the location of the tree. Physical limits on the maximum diameter of a tree trunk and the height of a tree bound the distance that the tree could possibly be from the camera. The tree's image and the distance constraints form a bounded cone in space that is stored as the location of the tree. This relatively large volume can be reduced when additional contextual knowledge is available, such as the maximum height of any tree in the immediate vicinity.

Once the distance to the tree is known, its height, width, and trunk diameter can be estimated. These estimates are stored in the database along with other attributes of the object's appearance for later use.

A second issue that must be resolved is the *reference problem*. Given a database of objects and an image of some of them, how can the correspondence between image and database models be established? This is a thorny philosophical issue when pursued to the extreme. For our purposes, we exploit the fact that the objects recognized by Condor are for the most part stationary, and we ignore the possibility that, for example, a tree has been removed and replaced with a different one. The strategy employed by Condor is simply that whenever an image feature could possibly refer to a given database object, it is assumed to do so. This sometimes results in images of two different trees corresponding to the same tree model in the database, but the error can be corrected when an image that disambiguates the situation is eventually analyzed.

After analyzing each image, Condor updates the CKS database to reflect its findings. By incrementally adding to this description of the environment, Condor learns the identity, location, size, shape, and appearance of most of the objects in its vicinity.

4.4.2   APPLYING RECOGNITION PROCEDURES MORE EFFECTIVELY

One of the primary goals for the Condor architecture was to exploit contextual information during the recognition process. Thus, as the CKS database is populated, Condor not only learns the layout of objects in the environment, but also learns how to recognize other objects.

Condor uses three mechanisms to learn how to recognize objects better using its existing context rules.

Same object, different image:

Whenever an object is recognized, it is stored in the CKS database. In addition to its location and physical attributes, Condor also stores the name of the operator and the associated parameters that extracted the region. When presented with a new image, Condor retrieves from the database all objects in the target vocabulary that lie within the field of view. For each such object, Condor determines the operator(s) that have successfully extracted the object in a previous image. These operators are applied to the new image, even if their context sets would not otherwise be satisfied. The results are treated as any other candidate hypothesis would be, but their inclusion can be responsible for successful recognition. This implements the strategy "If it worked once, it just might work again."

Different object, same class:

It is often the case that similar objects in a limited vicinity have a similar appearance. To exploit this observation, Condor has been provided with a class of operators designed to find similar candidates. When a candidate is accepted into a clique, a Type I context rule such as

> BUSH:　{ LAST-CANDIDATE-IS(bush) }　⟹
> opSIMILAR-REGIONS(intensity, vegetative-texture)

is invoked that attempts to find other regions in the same image that are similar in appearance to the one already accepted. For example, additional bush candidates are generated by finding regions that are within one standard deviation of both the INTENSITY and VEGETATIVE-TEXTURE measure of the (tentatively) known bush.

Similarity is also used for evaluating candidates. For example, if there is already a sky candidate in a clique, then the following Type II context rule

> SKY :　{ CLIQUE-CONTAINS(sky) ∧ RGB-IS-AVAILABLE }　⟹
> SIMILAR-COLOR(sky)

is employed to determine how closely each new candidate resembles the region already determined to be sky. The algorithm employed uses a histogram matching technique similar to that described by Swain [1990]. In the univariate case, we compute the histograms $H_M(i)$ and $H_C(i)$ of the known model and the candidate respectively. The similarity between a model region M and a candidate region C is given by computing the RMS difference between the cumulative histograms:

$$\sigma(H_M(i), H_C(i)) = 1 - \sqrt{\frac{1}{n} \sum_{i=0}^{n} [NCH_M(i) - NCH_C(i)]^2} \qquad (4.1)$$

where n is the number of buckets in the histogram and $NCH(i)$ is the normalized cumulative histogram defined by

$$NCH(i) = \frac{\sum_{j=0}^{i} H(j)}{\sum_{j=0}^{n} H(j)} . \qquad (4.2)$$

This is better suited for our purposes than Swain's method, which does not use cumulative histograms, because it does not overly penalize similar histograms that are offset slightly.

This method is also used to compute similarity based on several attributes simultaneously, such as the three bands of a color image, or intensity and texture together. In this case the multidimensional normalized cumulative histograms are computed as

$$NCH(x, y, z) = \frac{\sum_{i=0}^{x} \sum_{j=0}^{y} \sum_{k=0}^{z} H(i, j, k)}{\sum_i \sum_j \sum_k H(i, j, k)} \qquad (4.3)$$

and the similarity is computed using the obvious extension of Equation (4.1).

Candidate comparison uses this measure of similarity as one of the metrics for constructing partial orders. As a result, candidates that are very similar in appearance to those already in the cliques tend to rise toward the tops of the partial orders. This strategy could be summarized as "After recognizing an object, look for other features that are similar in appearance."

Different object, different class:

Because contextual information is of great value to Condor in recognizing objects, anything that is recognized is context for potential use by Condor. This affords an opportunity for Condor to bootstrap its recognition abilities. For example, recognizing a patch of **grass** allows Condor to infer where the **ground** is in an image. This may lead to a **tree-trunk** candidate being accepted into a clique because it can now be established to be supported by the **ground**. That **tree-trunk** may finally be interpreted to be part of a **tree** that was not previously in the database.

Furthermore, when a new image is acquired and that same tree is in the field of view, Condor will employ an operator that looks in a specific location for a pair of vertical edges that may delineate the trunk:

TREE-TRUNK: { USING-STORED-KNOWLEDGE, IN-FIELD-OF-VIEW(tree) }
$$\Longrightarrow \text{TREE-TRUNK-SNAKE}$$

The stored location, trunk diameter, and height are used as initial conditions for invoking the operator which optimizes the fit of a deformable model, as in Kass's snakes [Kass, Witkin, and Terzopoulos 1987]. This approach delineates the desired trunk whenever the location is known with sufficient accuracy.

Condor also uses the CKS database to help rank candidates. For example, the Type II context rule

TRAIL: { USING-STORED-KNOWLEDGE, IN-FIELD-OF-VIEW(trail) }
$$\Longrightarrow \text{COINCIDES-WITH-KNOWN(trail)}$$

is employed to measure the amount of overlap between a **trail** candidate and any known trails in the field of view. Candidates that do overlap significantly percolate to the tops of the partial order, where they are nominated for inclusion in a clique before other candidates. This implements a strategy that could be summarized as "Try to recognize known objects before considering other possibilities."

4.4.3 REFINING CONTEXT SETS

The use of a uniform representation of visual recognition knowledge in the form of context sets provides an opportunity to introduce a learning component within the Condor architecture. It should be possible to update the context sets automatically by retaining those that give generally reliable results and modifying or discarding those that do not. The practical impediments to learning discussed earlier have prevented us from employing an algorithm that automatically modifies Condor's knowledge base, but we remain optimistic that one could be incorporated. Several issues are involved.

Concept formation:

The construction of a context set knowledge base can be viewed as a *concept formation problem* [Genesereth and Nilsson 1987]. Genesereth and Nilsson define a concept formation problem as a tuple, $\langle P, N, C, \Lambda \rangle$, where P is a set of positive instances of a concept, N is a set of negative instances, C is the set of concepts to be used in defining the concept, and Λ is the language to be used in phrasing the definition.

In our case positive and negative instances are provided by a canonical interpretation of the image. In a supervised learning mode, the positive instances are those candidates that are consistent with a (subjective) labeling provided by a human and the negative instances are all other candidates. In an unsupervised learning mode, the best clique is assumed correct and its component candidates form the set of positive instances.

The set of concepts C is given by the context elements CE_i together with the set of available operators when attempting to learn Type I context rules. For Type II context rules, the set C is given by the context elements and the set of evaluation metrics.

The language Λ is given by the syntax of a context rule:

$$L : \{CE_1, CE_2, \cdots, CE_n\} \Longrightarrow A \ .$$

In other words, Λ is the set of conjunctions of any number of context elements with one operator or evaluator.

Note that the vast majority of literature in machine learning (for example [Mitchell 1978]) deals with situations in which each instance is either positive or negative (i.e., the sets P and N are disjoint). In object recognition, ambiguity occurs frequently, and the sets P and N may overlap. Furthermore, the classical learning paradigm seeks a definition that is exact; that is, it exactly separates all instances into the sets P and N. Because of the built-in ability of the Condor architecture to achieve robust recognition in the face of an imperfect knowledge base, it is not necessary to derive context rules that are perfect discriminators.

Collecting statistics:

Regardless of the particular learning algorithm employed, it will be necessary to collect some form of statistics on the performance of Condor. In the case of Type I context rules, several useful tables could be constructed. The utility of a context rule

$$L : CS_i \implies Op_j$$

could be computed as a function

$$f(\ \text{Acc}(Op_j, CS_i),\ \text{Gen}(Op_j, CS_i),\ \text{Freq}(CS_i))$$

where

$\text{Acc}(Op_j, CS_i)$ is the number of correct candidates generated by Op_j when CS_i was satisfied;

$\text{Gen}(Op_j, CS_i)$ is the total number of candidates generated by Op_j when CS_i was satisfied; and

$\text{Freq}(CS_i)$ is the number of times that CS_i was satisfied.

This function would reward operators with a high acceptance rate and discount context sets CS_i that seldom arise. The goal of the learning algorithm then, is to find a collection of context rules that maximizes the sum of the utilities of the rules. Accomplishing this task is difficult because of the combinatorics in the number of potential context sets.

We have implemented a simplified version of this algorithm which keeps track only of the acceptance rate of each operator without regard to satisfaction of context elements. The cumulative reliability of each operator in generating accepted candidates is computed and updated whenever Condor analyzes an image. This reliability is used as one of the heuristics when deciding which candidate is to be nominated for inclusion into a clique. Generally, the candidate generated by the operator with the highest reliability is chosen. This strategy helps build good cliques early by preventing unlikely candidates from contaminating a clique before they can be determined to be inconsistent.

Context trees:

Instead of attempting to explore all potential context sets, it is possible to modify a given knowledge base incrementally with the goal of improving its performance. In one such algorithm that we have investigated, the context rules are encoded as context trees. As an example, Figure 4.15 denotes the four Type I context rules shown for generating bush candidates.

After each image is analyzed, Condor updates the statistics for each branch of the context tree, recording how often that branch was invoked

Class	Context elements	Operator
BUSH	SITE-IS(Stanford-hills) ∧ CAMERA-IS-HORIZONTAL	VEGETATIVE-TRANSPARENCY
BUSH	SITE-IS(Stanford-hills) ∧ ¬ CAMERA-IS-HORIZONTAL	DARK-REGIONS
BUSH	¬ SITE-IS(Stanford-hills)) ∧ IN-FIELD-OF-VIEW(bush)	ACTIVE-CONTOUR-MODEL(bush)
BUSH	¬ SITE-IS(Stanford-hills) ∧ ¬ IN-FIELD-OF-VIEW(bush)	SEGMENTATION-REGIONS

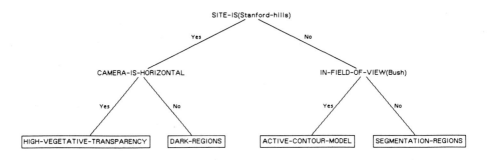

FIGURE 4.15. A context tree for generating bush candidates.

and how often it generated a candidate accepted by the best clique. When the reliability of any branch drops too low, a new context element that helps discriminate between positive and negative instances is added to the branch and operators for the two new leaf nodes are proposed. Devising optimal criteria for selecting new context elements and operators remains an open issue. In the example of Figure 4.15, the repeated failure of the DARK-REGIONS operator may cause the context tree to grow to that shown in Figure 4.16.

Branches that are seldom satisfied can be pruned from the context tree. After analyzing many images, the context tree could be expected to evolve into a knowledge base with an improved ability to generate good candidate hypotheses.

4.4.4   DISCOVERING NEW PROCEDURES

Ideally, a visual recognition system would be able to adapt its behavior to any environment with only a temporary degradation of competence. In Condor this would require adapting the operators, evaluators, and consistency determination routines to suit the new environment. While some improvement could be gained by reconfiguring the context sets, it should not be expected that Condor's current suite of procedures is adequate for domains much different from the foothills environment for which it was constructed. The procedures invoked by context rules are not in a declarative form, and it is hard to imagine how new visual operators could be generated automatically.

4.5   Complexity analysis

In the region-based approach to machine vision, an image is partitioned into r disjoint regions and a program must decide which of l potential labels to assign to each region. Because these assignments cannot be made independently, there are l^r potential labelings of the image from which the program must select the best.

In the model-based approach the regions associated with each model class are to be determined. Given l model classes and r possible locations of each model instance, there are r^l potential configurations of model instances in the worst case. (See Tsotsos [1988] for further elaboration.)

Class	Context elements	Operator
BUSH	SITE-IS(Stanford-hills) ∧ CAMERA-IS-HORIZONTAL	VEGETATIVE-TRANSPARENCY
BUSH	SITE-IS(Stanford-hills) ∧ ¬ CAMERA-IS-HORIZONTAL ∧ RGB-IS-AVAILABLE	GREEN-REGIONS
BUSH	SITE-IS(Stanford-hills) ∧ ¬ CAMERA-IS-HORIZONTAL ∧ RGB-IS-AVAILABLE	DARK-REGIONS
BUSH	¬ SITE-IS(Stanford-hills) ∧ IN-FIELD-OF-VIEW(bush)	ACTIVE-CONTOUR-MODEL(bush)
BUSH	¬ SITE-IS(Stanford-hills) ∧ ¬ IN-FIELD-OF-VIEW(bush)	SEGMENTATION-REGIONS

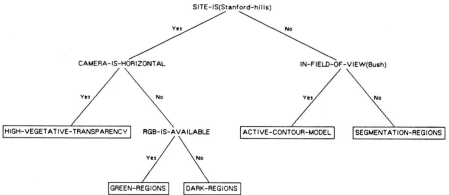

FIGURE 4.16. Modified context tree for generating bush candidates.

Most, if not all, of the existing systems for recognition can be viewed as strategies to explore either of these exponential search spaces. In contrast, Condor defines an entirely different search space — one that is polynomial in both the number of regions and the number of labels being considered — by identifying and exploring only the most promising portions of the space.

4.5.1 MATHEMATICAL DETAILS

To compute the computational complexity of the Condor architecture, it is convenient to characterize the algorithm as repeatedly testing candidates for consistency with a partially instantiated clique. At each stage, Condor must generate new candidates, update the partial orders, select a candidate for inclusion, and test it for consistency with the clique. In practice, Condor rarely needs to generate many new candidates after the initial iteration, but for analyzing worst-case complexity, we will assume that it does. Let

$$l \quad = \quad \text{the number of labels in the recognition vocabulary}$$

$$c \quad = \quad \text{the number of candidates for each label}$$

$$r \quad = \quad \text{the number of candidate regions in the largest clique}$$

$$q \quad = \quad \text{the total number of cliques constructed.}$$

At most, Condor must construct a total of lc candidates. Completely re-building each partial order requires c^2 operations, so lc^2 operations are required for partial order construction in the worst case. Selecting a candidate from the tops of the partial orders is no worse than linear in the number of candidates and testing for consistency could require as many as r tests. The maximum number of operations required for one complete iteration is

$$2lc + lc^2 + r \ . \tag{4.4}$$

This cycle must be repeated for each of the r candidates introduced into the clique. Completely repeating the process for q cliques is not necessary, but would require

$$(2lc + lc^2 + r)rq \tag{4.5}$$

operations. Therefore, the worst-case complexity for analyzing one image is

$$\mathcal{O}(qr^2 + lrqc^2) \ . \tag{4.6}$$

Formula 4.6 gives the total time complexity for analyzing one image and yields two important observations:

- Despite the combinatorics inherent in the recognition problem, our approach has no exponential behavior. The complexity is only quadratic in the number of regions to be recognized. This behavior is attributable to the fact that Condor constructs a fixed number of cliques and does not exhaustively search the exponential recognition space. While there is no guarantee that Condor will find the optimal clique, the context-based generation and relative ordering of candidates ensure that only good cliques are generated early in the search.

- The complexity is linear in the number of terms in the recognition vocabulary. Therefore, expanding the system by adding additional categories to be recognized results only in a proportional increase in run time. This behavior is important because it allows Condor to be expanded to recognize a broad range of categories without a prohibitive increase in computation. We know of no other visual recognition system that possesses this property.

4.5.2   THE NUMBER OF CLIQUES

The key to achieving desirable computational complexity is to accept candidates into cliques with sufficient reliability that the best clique is found early in the search. How reliable must candidate acceptance be?

Let p be the probability that a candidate nominated for inclusion into a clique is a member of the best clique (i.e., the label associated with the candidate is correct).[4] The probability of constructing a clique with r valid regions is p^r. On average, it will be necessary to construct $q = \frac{1}{p^r}$ cliques before the best one is found. Thus, if the best clique is to be found within the first q cliques, it will be necessary that

$$p \geq q^{\frac{-1}{r}} \ .$$

This relation is plotted in Figure 4.17 assuming that 40 regions are in the best clique. From the graph it is clear that candidate acceptance must be

---

[4]We assume for this analysis that the probability is the same for all nominated candidates.

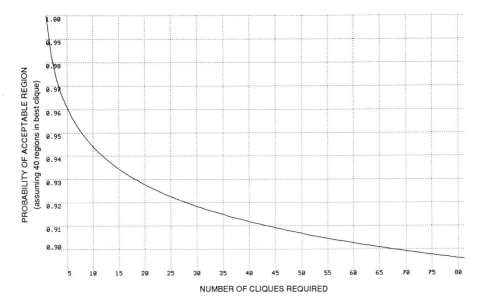

FIGURE 4.17. Graph of probability that a candidate is correct vs. number of cliques that would have to be generated to find the best clique.

perfect if only one clique is to be generated. If 95% reliability is attainable, then 7 cliques would be required; if only 90% reliability were attainable, then 68 cliques would be needed.

Although most of the operations employed by Condor are individually unreliable, their collective use is highly reliable. For example, in the course of analyzing the image in Figure 2.3, candidates that were accepted into cliques were 98% correct, based on a subjective assessment of which candidates were valid. At other stages of the analysis,

- 53% of the candidates generated by the context sets were valid.

- 78% of the candidates at the tops of the partial orders were valid.

- 82% of the candidates nominated for inclusion were valid.

- 98% of the candidates accepted by the consistency checking context sets to any clique were valid.

- 100% of the candidates in the best clique were valid.

In summary, the control structure limits the complexity of the approach:

- Because hypothesis generation is context-sensitive, the only operators that are employed are those that can be reasonably expected to succeed.

- Partial order construction is performed so that the most likely candidates are considered first and unlikely ones need never be considered.

- Global consistency is used as the basis for pruning large portions of the search space that would be explored by systems employing only local methods.

4.6   Discussion

4.6.1   RELIABILITY

One of the implicit goals in formulating the Condor architecture was to achieve reliable recognition despite the complexity of ground-level imagery of the outdoor world. Based on our empirical results, we find that Condor seldom misclassifies an object, but on occasion will leave a feature unlabeled or labeled with a general term high in the abstraction hierarchy. The most desirable stance on this tradeoff between complete labeling and avoidance of error depends on the intended task. For autonomous navigation, it is preferable to insist upon reliable labelings at the expense of completeness. Therefore, Condor has been designed to minimize the chance of an incorrect label and to rely on subsequent images to resolve unlabeled features.

Four features of the architecture are responsible for the reliability that Condor has demonstrated:

Redundancy — By employing many procedures designed to achieve the same result but using different means, Condor increases the chance that at least one of them will succeed.

Use of context — By employing procedures only in situations where they are likely to succeed, Condor reduces the chance that the procedure will fail. Furthermore, by constructing a model of objects in the world, Condor needs to recognize an object only once; it can verify that existence thereafter.

Global constraint — By allowing partial recognition results throughout the image to constrain an interpretation, Condor reduces its dependence on local peephole-type operations that are prone to failure.

Simplicity — Because the transition from signal to symbols in the generate-evaluate-test paradigm is short, there are fewer opportunities for error than in recognition paradigms that involve many transformations from image feature to 3D interpretation.

4.6.2   RECOGNITION STRATEGIES

Many approaches to computer vision can be categorized as top-down (model driven) or bottom-up (data driven). Condor's control structure blends several strategies into a uniform architecture for visual recognition:

Bottom-up — Objects with distinctive features can be delineated by context rules tailored to find those features.

Top-down — The 3D world model maintained by Condor is used to predict the location and appearance of objects in a model-based fashion.

Lateral — Context rules tailored to find candidates similar to those already recognized provide an additional strategy for identifying features within an image.

Tracking — Condor tracks objects through temporal image sequences by predicting the location and appearance of objects in the world model and verifying their existence.

The presence of all these strategies in a common framework allows Condor to employ those that work best in any given situation and to switch among them as circumstances dictate. Rather than hard-coding the recognition strategy in a vision program, we allow context to select the appropriate strategy for Condor.

4.6.3   KNOWLEDGE-BASE CONSTRUCTION

Machine vision algorithms can be very reliable when invoked in specific contexts in which all their assumptions are known to be satisfied. However, if these contexts are defined too narrowly, they will seldom arise. Constructing the context set knowlege base for Condor demands addressing this tradeoff between the specificity of a context set and the frequency of its occurrence.

If contexts are defined too narrowly, an enormous number of rules will be required. If contexts are defined too broadly, their associated operations will be unreliable. One of our hypotheses has been that it is possible to find procedures that work well in sufficiently broad contexts such that at least one will succeed in nearly every context that could arise. While we cannot offer proof that this is the case, it has been our experience that the number of new procedures required has decreased dramatically as additional images have been presented to Condor. Whether this need for new procedures decreases asymptotically to zero remains unknown. If so, it can be expected that a knowledge base of modest size will be sufficient for recognition in a given domain; if not, it will be necessary to employ automated knowledge acquisition to continually amend the knowledge base to match the requirements of the current site.

4.6.4   MULTIPLE-IMAGE INTERPRETATION

Condor has been designed to use a terrain database (CKS) to aid its interpretation of an image, and then to store its recognition results in that database. The emphasis has been on the use of the terrain database as contextual knowledge to support machine vision, but the maintenance of that database is equally important if the results from the interpretation of multiple images are to be correlated.

One issue that arises is the association of candidates with objects in the database. Candidates that are generated by verifying the presence of something already in the database are assumed to refer to that database object. For other candidates, the matching of accepted candidates to database objects can be problematic. Condor exploits the opinion mechanism of the CKS to resolve this. Rather than attempt to solve the reference problem, Condor simply stores a recognized object in the CKS as the opinion of the image in which it was found.

This strategy simplifies Condor's storage requirements, but permits some objects to be represented multiple times. Because Condor uses the terrain database only to help it generate hypotheses, the only ramification of this will be the generation of some additional hypotheses.

For other purposes, such as path planning, a more consistent representation of the environment is necessary. It should be possible to design and implement a meta-process which oversees the database, attempting to singularize multiple instances of an object using knowledge of the timing and resolution of each image that posited an object in the database. Accounting for Condor's known failings and the behavior of objects over time should permit an acceptable resolution to the reference problem, but this has not been done. Condor simply adds new opinions to the CKS terrain database, never retracting an opinion or collapsing several opinions into a single one.

5

EXPERIMENTAL RESULTS

The approach to machine vision that we have described is an attempt to overcome some of the fundamental limitations that have hindered progress in image understanding research. The ideas designed into that architecture embody a theory of computational vision for complex domains. To evaluate that theory, it is necessary to define a goal and to perform experiments that test how well the theory achieves that goal.

5.1 Evaluation scenario

In Section 3.1, we described a scenario in which an autonomous vehicle explores a piece of terrain by interpreting imagery obtained by an on-board camera. The vision system is to derive sufficient information from the imagery to enable the vehicle to navigate through the environment safely and efficiently. It should avoid real obstacles such as trees and large rocks, but not be deterred by insubstantial obstacles such as bushes and tall grass. Doing this requires recognition of several natural classes and would provide the data necessary for a navigation system to plan an intelligent route through the terrain for almost any type of mobility platform on which it is mounted.

To evaluate the Condor approach we have designed and implemented a knowledge base of context rules tailored to recognizing natural objects in a limited area. We have selected a two-square-mile region of foothills on the Stanford University campus as our site for experimentation. This area contains a mixture of oak forest and widely scattered oak trees distributed across an expanse of gently rolling, grass-covered hills and is criss-crossed by a network of trails. An aerial photograph and the corresponding portion of a USGS map depicting the region appear in Figure 5.1.

The ultimate challenge would be to develop a visual recognition system that could reliably recognize instances of a target vocabulary from

(a) Aerial photograph of experimentation site

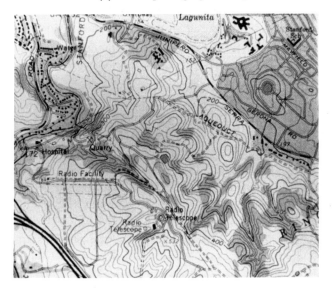

(b) USGS map of
the same area

FIGURE 5.1. Aerial photograph and map of the Condor experimentation site.

any non-degenerate image acquired within the region. Practical considerations prevent us from thoroughly testing how closely Condor achieves this goal, but the results presented here and elsewhere [Strat and Fischler 1989, Strat and Fischler 1990] should attest to the degree to which progress has been made. Perhaps more important is our belief that this goal is achievable by extending the knowledge base without making significant change to the architecture.

We have chosen 14 classes for recognition on the basis of their prevalence in the experimentation site and their importance for navigation. These terms are:

- **Geometric horizon** — the line in the image where the skyline would appear if the world were flat and level.

- **Complete sky** — the portion of the image where the sky would appear if all raised objects were removed.

- **Complete ground** — the portion of the image where the ground would appear if all raised objects were removed.

- **Skyline** — the boundary between **complete sky** and **complete ground**.

- **Sky** — that portion of the image which portrays the sky or clouds.

- **Ground** — the earth's surface or any object such as grass, leaves, or dirt that lie on it.

- **Raised object** — any object that protrudes above the surface of the ground.

- **Foliage** — any vegetation comprised of branches and/or leaves.

- **Bush** — any foliage that has no discernible trunk.

- **Tree trunk** — that part of a tree that extends from the ground to the crown.

- **Tree crown** — the foliage suported by a tree trunk.

- **Tree** — any foliage with a discernible trunk.

- **Trail** — an elongated, unvegetated portion of the ground that would be reasonable for a person to walk on.

- **Grass** — any portion of the ground that is predominantly covered by grass.

Procedures have been devised to extract, evaluate, and check the consistency of candidates for each of these classes. Context sets have been constructed to control the invocation of each of those procedures. Currently the knowledge base contains 88 procedures whose invocation is governed by 156 context sets. All the results presented in this document have been generated using this knowledge base or a subset of it.

Initial contextual information was extracted from the USGS map and the aerial photograph. In particular, we have made use of a 30-meter-grid digital terrain model, the road network, and the location of forested regions as shown on the map. The aerial photo, being more recent, was used to update the map information. These data were extracted by hand and stored in the Core Knowledge Structure.

Over 200 images have been acquired from the experimentation site, nearly half of which have been digitized and analyzed by Condor. Included in this image set are binocular stereo pairs obtained with a binocular camera and color images in addition to monochrome intensity data. Most images were digitized at a resolution between 250 and 1000 pixels on a side. The following sections detail the results obtained by applying Condor to the analysis of these images.

Three experiments have been devised to test the validity of the following hypotheses:

- The Condor architecture is suitable for recognizing natural objects in many contexts.

- A geographic database of an extended region can be constructed by combining the recognition results from several images.

- Using context allows Condor to learn how to recognize natural objects.

While none of these conjectures can be proved conclusively, the results of our experimentation provide strong evidence of their validity.

5.2 Experimentation

The research results presented here are indicative of the performance of Condor when analyzing scenes from the Stanford experimentation site. By themselves, these results do little to endorse the Condor approach, but together with similar results that have been obtained with several dozens of other images, they attest to the validity of the ideas contained therein. The cases that are presented have been chosen because they exemplify the capabilities and limitations inherent in the Condor architecture. These results are summarized but not presented in detail because of the space required by a full description.

5.2.1 EXPERIMENT 1

One shortcoming of many machine vision systems is their brittleness when analyzing scenes that exhibit significant variance in the setting or appearance of their components. Our design has attempted to relax this restriction because natural scenes possess great variability. How well we have achieved this goal can be assessed by testing the following claim:

Hypothesis 1 *The Condor architecture is suitable for recognizing natural objects in many contexts.*

In this experiment, Condor analyzed images taken under a variety of conditions at the Stanford experimentation site. These images were selected to study how Condor deals with changes in scale, view angle, time of day, season, cloud cover, and other ordinary changes that occur over the course of several years. Here we present a sample of those images that illustrates the breadth of competence exhibited by Condor.

Figure 5.2 shows four images of the same tree for which image acquisition parameters are given in Table 5.1. The field of view of each image is overlaid on the aerial photograph shown in Figure 5.3.

In all four of these images, Condor successfully identified the tree without the benefit of any prior information (Figure 5.4). In three of the images, the trunk was identified by a specialized operator designed to detect thin, dark, vertical lines. In the fourth image, one of Condor's wide-trunk detection algorithms (a variant of a correlation-based road-tracking algorithm) was responsible for generating the correct trunk. Given that context, Condor used several of its texture measures to help identify the foliage and assem-

FIGURE 5.2. Four images of the same tree as used in Experiment 1.

TABLE 5.1. Image acquisition parameters for images used in Experiment 1.

	upper-left	lower-left	lower-right	upper-right
range:	194 feet	56 feet	87 feet	28 feet
view angle:	160°	208°	258°	124°
date:	12 April 90	12 April 90	12 April 90	28 July 88

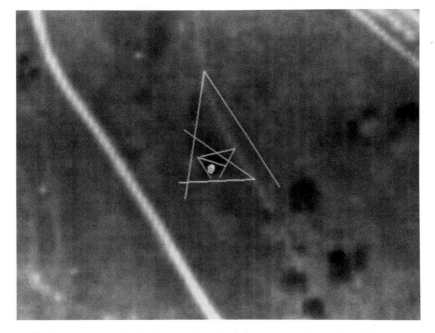

FIGURE 5.3. The field of view of each of the images depicted in Figure 5.2.

FIGURE 5.4. The models of the trees as they were recognized by Condor.

bled the results into 3D models to confirm the existence of the tree. These results illustrate Condor's abilities to recognize a tree from any view angle, to accommodate a 7:1 range in scale, to be immune from changes that occurred over a period of 21 months, and to deal with seasonal variation. When Condor has prior knowledge of the existence of this tree, it can be recognized from a distance of 590 feet (as demonstrated in Experiment 3), thereby extending its abilities to a 20:1 range in scale.

Experiments applying Condor to other images (not reproduced here) confirm the adequacy of the approach for recognizing natural objects in a wide variety of settings that occur at the experimentation site. The modularity of the context sets makes it possible to expand the breadth of competence still further without degrading previously demonstrated capabilities.

5.2.2   EXPERIMENT 2

To support autonomy in an intelligent, ground-based vehicle, it is necessary to synthesize a reasonably complete description of the entire surroundings, and not just recognize a few isolated objects. This description can be built incrementally because the world does not change very rapidly considering the spatial and temporal scales at which an autonomous ground vehicle would operate. The following hypothesis summarizes this notion:

Hypothesis 2 *A geographic database of an extended region can be constructed by combining the recognition results from several images.*

To test this hypothesis, a sequence of imagery was collected which simulates the movement of a vehicle through a portion of the Stanford experimentation site. The vision system is to construct a labeled, 3D map of the primary features in the vicinity of the simulated vehicle by analyzing each image in turn.

Figure 5.5 displays the eight images used in this experiment and Figure 5.6 shows the location of the vehicle when each was acquired. Condor was tasked to locate the trees, bushes, trails, and grass in each of these images, beginning with only the information extracted from the USGS map (Figure 5.7).

The results of Condor's analysis are portrayed in Figure 5.8. It would be exceedingly tedious to describe the complete sequence of computations that led to these results. Here we highlight a few of the more interesting chains of reasoning and explain the misidentifications that were made:

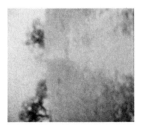

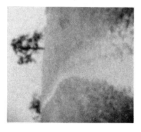

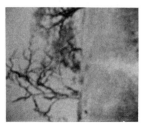

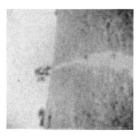

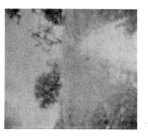

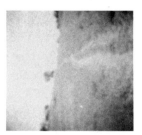

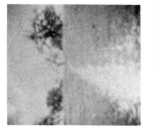

FIGURE 5.5. Sequence of eight images simulating the movement of a vehicle through the terrain.

FIGURE 5.6. The location and orientation of the camera when each image in Figure 5.5 was acquired.

FIGURE 5.7. Initial context used in Experiment 2.

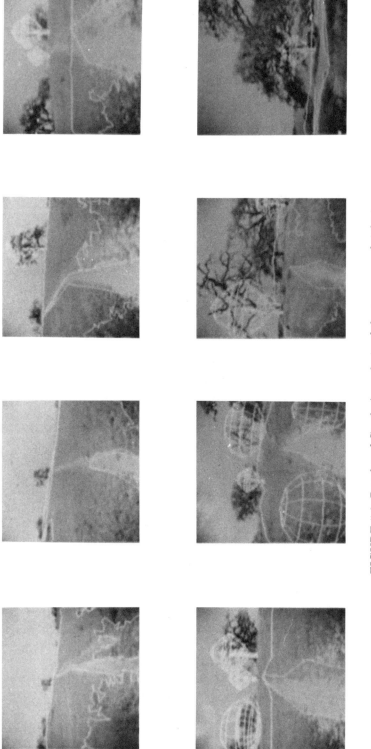

FIGURE 5.8. Results of Condor's analysis of the sequence of eight images.

Image 1 — Condor has correctly labeled the sky, the ground, the trail, and part of the grass, although the trees on the horizon were too indistinct to be reliably identified. These results are normally transformed into three-dimensional models using depth data acquired from binocular stereo or a laser rangefinder. In this example no range data were available, so Condor estimated the depths by projecting each region onto the USGS DTM. The resulting models were added to the CKS database to be used as context for the analysis of subsequent images.

Image 2 — The model of the trail from the first image was projected into the second image and used to help identify a portion of the trail. This is accomplished by an operator that superimposes a pair of parallel 3D curves and deforms them to find the model with maximum edge strength while minimizing its curvature. Statistics from the intensity and texture of the grass in the first image were used to help identify the grass in this image. In this case, the trail-finding operators failed to find the upper half of the trail; as a result, the grass hypotheses in that area were not contradicted.

Image 3 — The tree is finally close enough to allow reliable recognition and a 3D model for it is computed by extracting the envelope of its foliage. The distance to the tree is computed by projecting the base of the trunk onto the digital terrain model, and the resulting model is stored in the CKS. In this instance, the tree is actually situated just beyond the horizon on the back side of the hill. Condor is unaware of this and places the tree at the crest of the hill.[1] The entire visible portion of the trail was correctly identified.

Image 4 — Two additional trees are recognized and stored.

Image 5 — The same trees are recognized by predicting their location and verifying their existence — a much more reliable process than initially extracting them. No trunk was detectable in the foliage to the left of the image, so Condor labeled it as bush.

---

[1]More accurate placement might be achieved without range data by finding the tree in the aerial photo (Figure 5.1). The Condor approach might be applied to this subproblem, using operators that search along the ray from the camera center in the direction of the tree. This has not been implemented.

Image 6 — The texture in the lower corners of the sixth image was found to more closely resemble foliage than grass, so these regions were erroneously identified as bushes. Beause they are very near to the camera, they occupy a significant part of the image, but the 3D model created for them reveals that they are less than 2 feet tall.

Image 7 — Several more trees, grass areas, and part of the trail are recognized in the seventh image.

Image 8 — The primary tree is recognized despite the strong shadows, but the lower portion of the trunk was omitted by all the trunk operators. As a result, the tree is misplaced in the 3D model because the base of the detected trunk projects onto a distant ridge. Most of the tree crown operators were unable to provide a decent candidate because of the overhanging branches in the upper-right corner — the only operator that succeeded was the one that predicts the crown based on the size and location of the trunk. The combined effects of the incomplete trunk, the nearness of the tree, and the lack of range data account for the poor extraction of the tree crown. When Condor uses range data instead of the DTM positioning method, the tree is placed and sized correctly.

This experiment illustrates how Condor is able to use the results of analyzing one image to assist the analysis of other images. Although some trees and parts of the trail were missed in several images, the 3D model that results is nearly complete. Figure 5.9 shows an aerial view of the composite model contained in the CKS after processing all eight images. For comparison, Figure 5.10 portrays a hand-generated model of the objects actually present on the ground, constructed by physically measuring the locations and sizes of the individual objects. Note that all of the trees that were visible in at least one image have been correctly labeled, although some of them were misplaced by the DTM positioning method. Most of the trail has been detected; enough to allow a spatial reasoning process to link the portions into a single continuous trail. Furthermore, everything that was labeled **tree** actually is a tree.

This experiment demonstrates that Condor is able to construct a reasonably complete model of its vicinity by fusing the interpretation results from a sequence of images.

(a) Model constructed without benefit of range data

(b) Model constructed using simulated range data

FIGURE 5.9. The composite model resulting from the analysis of the image sequence in Figure 5.5.

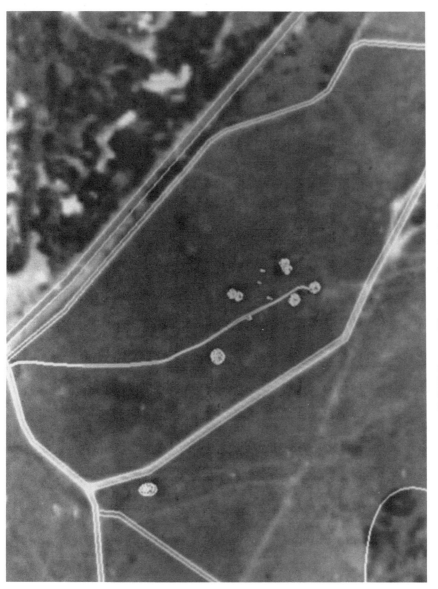

FIGURE 5.10. The ground-truth database.

5.2.3 EXPERIMENT 3

Regardless of the architecture, knowledge-based vision systems are difficult to build. If the programmer needed to specify in advance all the information necessary for successful recognition, his task would be hopeless. Therefore, it is essential that a vision system have the ability to improve its competence autonomously, thereby learning through experience how to recognize the objects in its environment. We wish to test whether the Condor architecture has an ability to learn from experience.

Hypothesis 3 *Using context allows Condor to learn how to recognize natural objects.*

To test this conjecture, we return to the first image of the sequence used in Experiment 2 (Figure 5.8). When originally analyzed, Condor recognized the trail and part of the grass, but not the trees. Can Condor extract enough information from other images to enable it to better interpret this image?

Condor was tasked to reanalyze the first image, this time making use of the contents of the entire database constructed as a result of processing the sequence of eight images. The resulting interpretation is depicted in Figure 5.11.

Two trees that could not be extracted on the first pass are now identified. Condor employed a tree-trunk operator whose context set requires knowledge of the approximate location of a tree in the field of view. The operator projects a deformable 3D model of the trunk onto the image, and optimizes its fit to extract the trunk. This operator successfully identified two of the trees without contradicting any of the original recognition results.

Figure 5.12 shows that Condor was also able to recognize a tree in the second image of the sequence as well. This tree was not recognizable without the models constructed by Condor during its prior analysis of the sequence.

This experiment illustrates that the ability to use prior recognition results as context while interpreting subsequent images enables Condor to improve its performance as its exposure to its environment increases.

5.3 Analysis of results

The experiments presented in the previous section reveal some of the capabilities and limitations of Condor. Two questions are explored here:

FIGURE 5.11. The results of analyzing the first image from Figure 5.5 with and without the information extracted from subsequent images.

FIGURE 5.12. The results of analyzing the second image from Figure 5.5 with and without the information extracted from subsequent images.

- When Condor makes an error, what has gone wrong, and how can it be fixed?

- What features of the architecture are responsible when Condor interprets a scene correctly?

5.3.1 FIXING MISTAKES

As demonstrated in the results presented in Section 5.2, Condor errs in its interpretation of some scenes. It is important to know the cause of such errors, to determine how difficult it would be to fix them.

A closer look at the mistakes made during the analysis of the sequence of eight images used in Experiment 2 (Figure 5.8) gives some insight into the cause of typical errors:

Image 1 — Although nothing was mislabeled, Condor only found several small patches of grass while the remainder of the hillside was labeled merely as ground. One operator uses known grass regions as models to identify other similar grass regions, but in this case the remainder of the hillside was too dissimilar. This illustrates an intrinsic conservatism in the approach, which attempts to avoid labeling something unless it is clearly supported. Knowledge of other examples of grass could be used as prototypes, and would allow Condor to extract these grass regions properly.

Image 2 — Only the lower half of the trail was recognized as trail. The operators used for generating trail hypotheses failed to produce candidates that included that part of the trail. As a result, grass candidates that overlapped the trail were not contradicted, and the upper part of the trail was mistakenly labeled as grass. This situation can be avoided by adding more capable trail operators that in this context could delineate the trail better, or by invoking the same operators with different parameter values.

Image 6 — Here, Condor hallucinated two small bushes on either side of the trail. The strong texture exhibited by the grass in the lower corners of the image caused these regions to be placed relatively low in the partial order of grass candidates. As a result, bush candidates at these locations tended to be accepted into cliques earlier than the competing grass candidates and remained in the final interpretation.

It is conceivable that if more cliques had been generated, a better interpretation without these bushes would have been obtained. A more direct way to fix the problem would be to add a Type II context rule that allows highly textured grass candidates in contexts in which they are very near to the camera. This would raise their position in the grass partial order and allow them to enter cliques before the mediocre bush candidates.

Image 8 — The tree is misplaced and undersized because of the unfortunate combination of several problems. The trunk extractors were confused by the strong shadow and missed the base of the trunk. One could envision improving the trunk operators, but it would probably be more efffective to add **shadow** to the recognition vocabulary, and to reason about shadows directly.

Each of these errors can be attributed to some shortcoming in the knowledge base of context rules employed in these experiments. When fixes are required, the following options are available:

- Adding a new operator

- Adding a new evaluation metric

- Adding a new consistency constraint

- Modifying the context set contained in an existing rule

Modifications have been suggested for correcting these mistakes and some have been implemented to avoid potential errors in similar cases. All of these problems can be fixed by refining the knowledge base without altering the architecture of the system. However, unless there is some assurance that additions to the knowledge base will not be needed indefinitely, there is the danger that the system will collapse from its sheer size, and sufficient recognition ability may never be achieved. While we cannot offer definitive evidence that this will not occur, it has been our experience that the frequency with which additional context rules have been needed has decreased dramatically as the knowledge base has grown. In fact, new images can usually be interpreted correctly using the existing knowledge base,

5.3.2 ACCOUNTING FOR SUCCESS

Analyzing the cause of errors provides guidance for improving the competence of the system. Analyzing the reasons that correct interpretations are made provides an understanding of the essential components of the system.

In order to gain an appreciation of the source of Condor's ability, the author conducted a series of ablation experiments in which some selected portion of the system was temporarily switched off and an analysis made of the resulting performance:

No use of context: Is the construction and use of a persistent world model worth the effort?

Experiment 3 showed several images in which some trees were recognized only after the world model had been constructed. Without access to that contextual information, Condor was unable to find the trees in Figures 5.11 and 5.12. This represents one pair of many examples in which Condor's ability can be traced directly to the use of information in the world model. Context is definitely important for recognition.

No partial orders: Is it necessary to order the candidates before forming cliques?

In this experiment, the Type II comparison context rules were not used, and all candidates were available for incorporation into cliques at the same time. Out of six images that were analyzed, none yielded a clique that was comparable to the best clique obtained with the use of the partial orders. In fact, up to 100 cliques were assembled for each image and most cliques so generated were incomplete or contained silly mistakes that are easily avoided through candidate comparison. The partial orders produced by Type II context rules are clearly an important component of the architecture.

No context sets: Is it necessary to use context to decide which procedures should be invoked?

In this experiment, Condor analyzed images while assuming that every context set was always satisfied and all procedures were employed. Some procedures failed simply because their preconditions were not met. Some hypothesis generators produced additional candidates that impaired efficiency but did not affect the final interpretation because other mechanisms in the architecture were able to eliminate them. The aditional candidate comparators that became available tended to conflict with those whose contexts were properly satisfied, yielding very flat partial orders that caused the same problems as having no partial orders. In conclusion, embedding context sets in rules to control the invocation of procedures is vital to the integrity of the system.

5.3.3   EVALUATING RELEVANCE TO THE GOAL

In summary, Condor appears to be well-suited for guiding the operation of an autonomous ground vehicle. The effects of the occasional misinterpretation are mitigated by the maintenance of a model of the environment that is incrementally updated. Even when mistakes are made, they are often of a type that is unlikely to affect safe navigation. The fictitious bushes that were identified in the sixth image of the sequence from Experiment 2 are small enough that they are unlikely to harm a vehicle. The trees that were missed in the first two images are sufficiently distant that they pose no immediate threat to the vehicle. Nearby portions of the trail, which are most important for navigation, are recognized much more reliably than distant ones.

6

CONCLUSION

6.1 Contribution

The key scientific question addressed here is the design of a computer vision system that can approach human-level performance in the interpretation of ground-level scenes of the natural world. Heretofore, no system has been constructed that demonstrates significant recognition competence in this domain and, worse, the field has not produced a theory about how such a system could be constructed. We offer a new paradigm for the design of computer vision systems that holds promise for achieving human-level competence, and report the experimental results of a system implementing that theory which demonstrates near-human recognition abilities in a natural domain of limited geographic extent.

Ground-level images of the natural world were chosen as the recognition domain for several reasons. The natural world is complex — natural features exhibit great variability in appearance from image to image, and defy compact description of their shapes. The natural world is thus a difficult visual domain, forcing the solution of fundamental problems rather than admitting to *ad hoc* solutions. The fact that biological visual systems evolved in a world of natural features and later adapted to the recognition of man-made artifacts lends credence to the belief that computer vision systems designed for the natural world may also be adapted to succeed in a manufactured domain. The converse is not true, and in fact there is much evidence that computer vision systems designed for other domains cannot be extended to understand images of the natural world. Finally, numerous potential applications could be enabled by the creation of a computer vision system for natural object recognition. Autonomous vehicles for the military, for the construction industry, and for agriculture are perhaps the most immediate uses of this technology.

When examining the reasons why the traditional approaches to computer vision fail in the interpretation of ground-level scenes of the natural world, four fundamental problems became apparent:

Universal partitioning: Most scene-understanding systems begin with the segmentation of an image into homogeneous regions using a single partitioning algorithm applied to the entire image. If that partitioning is wrong, then the interpretation must also be wrong, no matter how a system assigns semantic labels to those regions. Unfortunately, universal partitioning algorithms are notoriously poor delineators of natural objects in ground-level scenes.

Shape: Many man-made artifacts can be recognized by matching a 3D geometric model with features extracted from an image, but most natural objects cannot be so recognized. Natural objects are assigned names on the basis of their setting, appearance, and context, rather than their possession of a particular shape.

Computational complexity: The general recognition problem is NP-hard. As a result, computation time must increase exponentially as additional classes are added to the recognition vocabulary, unless a strategy to avoid the combinatoric behavior is incorporated. Such provisions are a necessary component of any recognition system that can be scaled to embrace a real domain.

Contextual knowledge: Despite the fact that recognition is an intelligent process requiring the application of stored knowledge, computer vision researchers typically use artificial intelligence techniques only at the highest levels of reasoning. The design of an approach that allows stored knowledge to control the lower levels of image processing has proved elusive.

A new paradigm for computer vision systems has been developed, which addresses all four of the problems described above. The key provision of this novel approach is a mechanism for the application of stored knowledge at all levels of visual processing. A context set, which explicitly specifies the conditions and assumptions necessary for successful invocation, is associated with every procedure employed by the recognition system.

The architecture is organized into three modules:

- Hypotheses concerning the presence in a scene of specific categories
  of objects are generated using special-purpose operators whose invocation is controlled by context sets, thereby avoiding the need for
  universal partitioning algorithms. This selective application of low-
  level operators produces high-quality hypotheses, which limits the
  combinatorics to be faced when searching for consistent sets (cliques)
  of hypotheses. The employment of large numbers of operators ensures
  that quality hypotheses can be generated in nearly every context and
  provides redundancy that decreases the reliance on the success of any
  individual operator.

- Candidates for each label are ranked so that the best ones can be
  tested for consistency before the others. This ensures that the largest
  consistent cliques will be found early in the search, and limits the
  computational complexity of the entire paradigm to a linear growth as
  the recognition vocabulary is expanded. By constructing only a small
  number of the most likely cliques for each image, the approach loses
  any guarantee of finding the largest clique, but assures the availability
  of a credible answer compatible with the computational resources of
  the system.

- Consistency is enforced by procedures (controlled by context sets)
  that detect and reject physically impossible combinations of hypotheses. The clique that most completely explains the available data is
  offered as the interpretation of an image. Thus, individual objects
  are labeled on the basis of their role in the context of the complete
  clique, rather than solely on the basis of individual merit.

The approach has been implemented in the form of a complete end-to-
end vision system, known as Condor. Images that may be monochromatic
or color, monocular or stereo, provide the input to the system, along with a
terrain database containing prior knowledge about the environment. Condor produces a 3D model of the environment, labeled with terms from its
recognition vocabulary. That model is used to update the terrain database
for use by Condor during the analysis of subsequent imagery.

A knowledge base of context sets and procedures was constructed for the
interpretation of ground-level images acquired from an undeveloped portion of the Stanford campus. Images representing a wide variety of viewing
conditions and seasonal variations have been analyzed by Condor. Exper-

imentation with these images reveals Condor's highly successful, although still imperfect, ability to recognize instances of 14 classes of natural features. The system has been used to construct a labeled 3D model of an environment by analyzing multiple ground level images such as shown in Figures 1.2 – 1.4. This model can be used in path planning and task exectution by an autonomous vehicle, and Condor has itself used this model to improve its own recognition abilities.

6.2 Evaluation

The evaluation of a computer vision system is a notoriously difficult endeavor. When semantic interpretation is involved, as in the Condor approach, there is no single correct answer to which results can be compared. Human vision is subjective and depends strongly on the assumed task, so that it is unclear how to determine whether a particular recognition result is or is not correct. Because there is no known mathematical or logical mapping from input image to recognition result, it is difficult to measure the performance of an approach analytically. Instead, as with any scientific theory, a computer recognition system must be tested empirically.

In this section, we informally evaluate the Condor approach along several dimensions and propose a plan that could be employed to evaluate Condor (and other recognition systems) through comparison of experimental results with human visual recognition.

6.2.1 COMPETENCE

Before a machine vision system can be employed as part of an autonomous vehicle or other host system, it must demonstrate an acceptable level of performance. Our current implementation of Condor does not have a sufficiently detailed repertoire of context sets and procedures for the general approach to be fairly evaluated, but a number of arguments can be made to show that the approach could achieve arbitrarily high reliability, at least in principle.

Contrary to conventional practice in computer vision, which attempts to design general-purpose approaches for recognition in as broad a range of contexts as possible, Condor provides a framework for applying different special-purpose procedures in different narrow contexts. Theoretically, one could achieve arbitrarily high reliability by adding a sufficient number of detailed context rules within Condor's knowledge base. Although this could conceivably require an indefinite number of rules, our experience has been that the number of additional context rules required to interpret new images decreased dramatically as the set of test images is expanded.

The Condor architecture incorporates four mechanisms whose primary purpose is to attain reliable recognition results, even in the presence of unreliable components:

- Control of procedures using context sets allows the invocation of only those procedures that have a significant chance of succeeding.

- The employment of large numbers of operators provides redundancy to increase the chance that at least one will generate a valid hypothesis in any circumstance.

- Evaluation of hypotheses is not performed on the basis of a single metric, but by the unanimous vote of many metrics.

- Recognition decisions are made for entire sets of consistent hypotheses, rather than individually.

6.2.2 SCALABILITY

A major concern with all recognition systems is how the performance changes as the system is scaled to larger domains. Performance can be characterized in many ways. In Section 4.5, the computational complexity of the approach was shown to increase only linearly as the recognition vocabulary is increased. Here we examine how the reliability of the interpretation can be expected to change as the recognition vocabulary is expanded.

Increasing the recognition vocabulary in Condor requires extending the abstraction hierarchy (Figure 3.1) by adding a term as a subclass of an existing term. For example, one could add pine and oak as subclasses of tree. Context rules must be created for generating, evaluating, and checking the consistency of pine and oak hypotheses, although appropriate ones can also be inherited from tree. Because of the modularity of the knowledge base, context rules for the other terms do not have to be modified.

Extending the vocabulary and its corresponding knowledge base is syntactically easy, although devising the new context rules may require a good deal of effort. How does such a vocabulary expansion (adding **oak** for example) affect the quality of the recognition?

The additional context rules will have no effect on other comparisons until an instance of the new class is added to a clique, thereby becoming part of the available context. Thus, candidates and partial orders for **oak** will be created, but previous computation paths are not changed.

Eventually, a candidate for the new label, say **oak**, will be accepted into a clique. If this oak happens to be one that would not have been identified as a tree without the resolution provided by the **oak** context rules, a ripple effect on other label hypotheses could occur:[1]

Candidate generation: Context sets for the generation of candidates for other terms, such as **tree-trunk**, could now become satisfied, causing the generation of new tree-trunk hypotheses.

Candidate evaluation: Candidates may now be ranked differently, given the presence of this oak in a clique, because additional metrics may become available through the satisfaction of previously unsatisfied context sets. Although earlier context sets do not reference oaks, Condor knows through the abstraction hierarchy that every oak is a tree (as well as a raised object).

Clique formation: The presence of an oak in a clique can have two effects on consistency determination. Other candidates may be found to be inconsistent with the oak, thereby eliminating some candidates that might otherwise have been accepted into the clique. Second, additional context sets for consistency-determination routines may become satisfied, thereby adding additional constraints for use in clique formation.

All of these changes may lead to results better or worse than those obtained before expanding the vocabulary. However, if all the context rules are reliable (i.e., the partial orders never rank an incorrect candidate above a correct one, and the consistency checks never allow an incorrect hypothesis into a clique), then the expanded knowledge base will only give a more

---

[1]This would not happen if the procedures associated with **tree** took full advantage of the available data (including the narrower context defined for oak trees).

complete interpretation of the scene. If this reliability assumption is correct, the incorporation of context rules for an additional term can only add to the already known context, which in turn could only cause more context sets to be satisfied, which could only improve the recognition result. In practice, this monotonicity is approachable, but cannot be guaranteed in general because it is unlikely that a completely reliable knowledge base could be built. For a single image however, if Condor attains a correct interpretation without the new vocabulary term, it will also attain a correct interpretation with the new term.

6.2.3   GENERALITY

The Condor knowledge base has been constructed to enable an autonomous vehicle to recognize objects at the Stanford experimentation site and the system has been demonstrated using imagery obtained there. What would happen if the vehicle were to wander beyond the experimentation site? What would be involved to employ Condor in a different domain?

The system can be divided into three components: the architectural framework, the knowledge base of context rules, and the terrain database.

- The architecture contains nothing that is peculiar to the Stanford site. In fact, it has been designed as a general theory for image interpretation in any complex domain. No changes should be necessary to adapt the architecture to a different domain.

- The knowledge base of context rules contains procedures and their associated context sets. The context sets can span the range from extremely specialized (e.g., horizontal camera, looking south, on a cloudy day, at the Stanford experimentation site) to the completely general (e.g., always). Certainly the rules with specialized context sets cannot be expected to perform well in other contexts, and indeed their procedures will not be invoked by Condor. The procedures with more general context sets may apply, but cannot be relied upon because they were designed without consideration for the unknown characteristics of hypothetical unforeseen domains. Thus, the context rules must be reexamined, and new ones added to deal with new or unanticipated domains. The collection of procedures will contain algorithms that are useful in other domains, but may require augmentation with additional procedures.

- The terrain database is not necessary for Condor's operation, but significantly improves its performance when available, as demonstrated in Experiment 3 (Section 5.2.3). It is always best to provide as much data as possible about a new environment, but Condor could walk off the edge of its terrain database and gradually extend the data through its own recognition results.

What domains other than ground-level natural scenes are suitable for analysis by Condor? The two most important characteristics of preferable domains are the following:

- It must be possible to construct procedures that delineate the desired features, although they need not be reliable. Only a small percentage of all hypotheses generated by these procedures must be correct. The domain of extracting buildings and roads from aerial imagery is probably well-suited for Condor, whereas the interpretation of ground-level scenes of the Martian surface, for which rock delineation is very difficult, is questionable.

- The domain must have sufficient contextual constraints. Interpretation of medical imagery in which anatomy provides strong constraint is probably well-suited for Condor. On the other hand, the industrial bin-of-parts problem provides insufficient contextual constraints.

6.2.4 EVALUATION PLAN

Direct comparison of the performance of two alternative approaches to natural object recognition would be desirable, but is impractical because computer vision systems are typically designed to function in distinct domains in support of different tasks; they cannot be evaluated independent of scene content or their supporting knowledge bases. The only currently feasible alternative is to compare a system's performance with human interpretation, despite the subjective nature of human vision.

Regrettably, the field of computer vision has yet to devise an accepted procedure for empirically evaluating the performance of its recognition systems. Here we propose a methodology for evaluating Condor, that might hold merit as an evaluation procedure for all recognition systems.

Our goal was to design an architecture that is able to represent and use visual knowledge of a limited geographic area so thoroughly that an autonomous vehicle could recognize everything relevant to its navigation and planning. The target vocabulary (Section 5.1) lists the classes of objects that have been deemed relevant and within the intended sphere of competence.

The proposed evaluation plan is as follows:

- The task to be evaluated is the identification of all instances of the target vocabulary in any image of a particular scene. The test images may be acquired over a period of time, exhibiting a range of viewing and environmental conditions, similar to the task employed in Experiment 1 (Section 5.2.1).

- The vision system designer will know the site in advance and have access to representative imagery. The actual images to be used in the test will not be made available beforehand. When ready for evaluation, the system must delineate each instance of the target vocabulary in each test image.

- The test images will also be given to a number of human subjects, who are to identify all instances of the target vocabulary in each image. They are to delineate each object as well as possible and name its class. All objects that are labeled identically by a preponderance of the human subjects (say 98%) will form the standard against which the computer vision system will be compared. Those objects that are not labeled or delineated consistently by nearly all the human subjects will not be considered during the evaluation.

- The comparison of computer and human performance will emphasize the accuracy of labeling and not the precision of delineation. Any object that is delineated approximately the same by both the machine and the human standard must be labeled the same. The fraction of correctly labeled objects is computed and used as the basis for assessing the performance of the system. The difference between this fraction and the percentage (98%) of human subjects who have agreed measures the degree to which human-level performance has been achieved.

This methodology provides an objective basis for evaluating a computer vision system, but requires substantial effort to invoke. Responses must be collected from a large number of people to ensure a statistically significant set of test data. Software must be written that allows the subject to enter delineations directly into the computer and that can decide when two delineations are substantially the same. These factors have so far precluded a formal evaluation of Condor and should be remedied in the future. The value to the field of computer vision warrants expenditure of substantial effort on a standard procedure for empirical evaluation such as the one described here.

In its present embodiment, Condor is still a demonstration system which should be evaluated primarily in terms of its architectural design and innovative mechanisms, rather than its absolute performance. While Condor has demonstrated a recognition ability approaching human-level performance on some natural scenes, it is still performing at a level considerably short of its ultimate potential (even for the Stanford experimentation site). The knowledge acquisition mechanisms, which are a key aspect of the architecture, should allow continued improvement in performance with exposure to additional site imagery.

6.3   Summary

Recognizing an object involves more than a simple classification based on measured features. It entails the use of contextual information and stored knowledge of the properties of the world, as well as the measured features, to properly interpret sensed data.

A new paradigm for image understanding has been proposed, and used to recognize natural features in ground-level scenes of a geographically limited environment. This context-based approach is exciting because it deemphasizes the role of image partitioning and emphasizes the recognition context in a way that has not been attempted before. This new focus could lead to the construction of vision systems that are significantly more capable than those available today.

Appendix A

THE CORE KNOWLEDGE STRUCTURE

This appendix describes an information storage and retrieval mechanism that avoids the requirement of consistency maintenance imposed by traditional knowledge-based systems. By viewing data as opinions rather than facts, the system is able to combine knowledge that is generally accepted as being true with data that may be from unreliable sources. A formal account of the semantics of the approach is described. The information management system has been implemented and used to store information derived from image processing along with opinions from other sources about objects in the visible world. It appears to be well-suited for the requirements of a vision system for an autonomous robot, and for information storage in general [Smith and Strat 1986].

A.1   Introduction

Database management systems are widely used to store and retrieve facts about the world. They provide a convenient and efficient means to access vast amounts of data and have been the basis of data management in many varied applications. In *knowledge-based systems* they have been used to manipulate data that encodes the knowledge that the system uses to carry out its activities. In these circumstances it has been usual to impose upon the data the requirement of consistency. The database is usually expected to be a consistent collection of facts presumed to be true about the world. Conflicting items of information are filtered from the database; else their presence would result in erroneous conclusions. For this reason, great care must be taken to ensure that false data is not inserted into the database and much effort has gone into developing procedures for ensuring the integrity of the data store. However, there are numerous knowledge-based system applications, autonomous robots being one, in which the requirement of database consistency is inappropriate.

Whenever information is provided by more than one source or when the validity of that information is undeterminable, it may be impossible to satisfy the requirements of consistency. For instance, suppose a friend tells us that the fishing in Lake Mohunk is great this time of year, and we wish to store this information in a database. We would first be obliged to ensure that it is not in conflict with anything already present in the database, and we would be required to ensure that that remains the case. In general, whether or not a statement is valid depends on a number of factors:

Credibility of the source – If our friend is an avid fisherman who just returned from the lake, we should be much more willing to accept his statement than if the source of information was hearsay.

Believability of the statement – If Lake Mohunk is the center of a fishing resort where fishing has been great in the past, we would likely accept our friend's statement readily; if it has been subject to pollution we would not.

Consistency with other statements – We would be unwilling to believe our friend if we had polled six fishermen and all the others told us that fishing at the lake is poor.

Intended use of the information – If we were just curious about our friend's recent fishing trip, we would have no reason to doubt his statement, but if we were planning a two-week vacation to Lake Mohunk, we might be unwilling to accept it without additional confirmation.

The traditional knowledge-based system design makes it difficult or impossible to take all these factors into account. We now describe an information storage system that was designed to overcome this limitation.

A.2 Core Knowledge Structure

The approach to database design we describe was motivated by the need to store information about the visual world in an autonomous robot. In particular, we have developed a Core Knowledge Structure (CKS) [Strat and Smith 1987a] to serve as a central information manager in a robot. A major component of CKS is a database that encodes the spatial and semantic properties and relations in the robot's environment. Because CKS accepts data from a wide variety of sources (vision and range sensors, maps, reasoning systems, and even humans), it is natural to expect that this information will be mutually inconsistent and error-prone.

The CKS database is a storehouse of the *opinions* of many agents. It is not a database of facts. This design has some unusual properties— properties that allow it to function as a central repository of information for a community of processes. It also renders much of the previous research in database designs inapplicable and has spurred us to develop new techniques for the storage and retrieval of multiple opinions.

The community of processes architecture adopted for the CKS requires that processes be able to communicate their opinions with one another and without undue interference from processes with competing views. The formalization and use of an opinion base in lieu of a database gives rise to the following important features:

- The ability to store information that is *inconsistent*.

- The ability to *integrate* multiple opinions and to allow that integration to depend upon the intended use of the information.

- The ability to *separate* one source's opinions from another's.

These goals have been achieved while retaining an ability to incorporate general knowledge that is universally accepted as being true. An opinion base appears to us to be a better model of how humans store information than a consistent database of facts.

A.3   Logical Interpretation of the CKS Database

Because of the presence of inconsistent information, first order logic is insufficient for describing the semantics of the database. In what follows, we will resort to a modal logic of belief as a means for interpreting CKS transactions. This logic is extremely expressive and could be used to specify a much richer collection of knowledge. However, we have purposely limited the scope of our logic as a concession to efficiency of implementation. We are, after all, designing the CKS as the core component of an autonomous vehicle, and implementation issues cannot be ignored. For this reason, the ultimate design is a compromise between the ability to express complicated statements involving beliefs of multiple agents and the ability to retrieve relevant information quickly. Throughout the design, we have been guided by the requirements of autonomous vehicles and have adopted what we feel to be an efficient implementation that does not sacrifice the ability to express the information that must be communicated among the various processes of an autonomous system.

A.3.1   SEMANTICS

Information is stored in the CKS in the form of data tokens. A *data token* is a framelike object whose internal structure is related to the semantic attributes of the object. Among other things, a data token contains information about the spatial location of an object and some domain-specific properties that are believed to be true about the object. For example, a portion of a data token, token01, might contain:

```
token01
  :SPATIAL-DESCRIPTION  (V1 V2)
  :SEMANTIC-DESCRIPTION (LARGE RED POST)
  :HEIGHT               7.3
     . . .
```

Here the *spatial description* is a list of volume specifications (as described in [Strat and Smith 1987a]) in which the object is presumed to lie. The *semantic description* is a list of properties that the asserting agent believes to be true about token01.

The precise meaning of CKS transactions is specified with the aid of modal logic. This logic consists of the following components:

Object Constants — The collection of all data tokens and potential data tokens in the database.

Function Constants — None.

Predicates — The set of vocabulary words and the set of possible spatial descriptions.

We adopt the usual syntax for forming well-formed formulas (WFFs) over these symbols as well as all the standard axioms of first order logic. In addition, we assume the existence of implicit axioms that allow us to

infer implicit spatial relationships and to make use of semantic relationships
encoded in a semantic network:

- $(\forall x)[V_i(x) \rightarrow V_j(x)]$

  whenever the volume denoted by V_i is completely contained within
  the volume denoted by V_j, where V_i and V_j are spatial descriptions.

- $(\forall x)[W_i(x) \rightarrow W_j(x)]$

  whenever W_i and W_j are connected by a 'subset' relation in the semantic network.

- $(\forall x)[W_i(x) \rightarrow \neg W_j(x)]$

  whenever W_i and W_j are connected by a 'disjoint' relation in the
  semantic network.

We employ a modal operator $\mathbf{B}_i$ to be interpreted as meaning
"agent i believes that" so that $\mathbf{B}_i[\Phi]$ is interpreted as "Process i believes Φ is true." This operator is similar to that described by Moore
[Moore and Hendrix 1979] and by Konolige [Konolige 1984]. However, our
axiomatization is different, as we only develop here those formulas that are
needed to interpret the action of the database.

The following axiom schema provides the modal operator with the semantics we desire:

- $\Phi \rightarrow \Psi \Rightarrow \mathbf{B}_i[\Phi] \rightarrow \mathbf{B}_i[\Psi]$ — The modal operator $\mathbf{B}_i$ is closed under
  deductive inference.

Significantly, this axiomatization does not require that $(\mathbf{B}_i[\Phi] \vee \mathbf{B}_i[\neg\Phi])$
is true, nor does it require that $(\mathbf{B}_i[\Phi] \wedge \mathbf{B}_i[\neg\Phi])$ is false. However, it
does require $(\mathbf{B}_i[\Phi] \vee \neg\mathbf{B}_i[\Phi])$ to be true and $(\mathbf{B}_i[\Phi] \wedge \neg\mathbf{B}_i[\Phi])$ to be false.
This arrangement allows conflicting beliefs to exist without corrupting the
database.

For any proposition Φ, an agent may have any of four states of belief.
These are listed below. An example is given of an English statement that
would be encoded by each of these states of belief. In the example $\Phi \equiv$
$House(\text{object})$, and $\forall x \, Car(x) \Longrightarrow \neg House(x)$ is included in the semantic
network:

- "The object is a house." $(\mathbf{B}_i[\Phi] \wedge \neg\mathbf{B}_i[\neg\Phi])$
- "The object is a house and it's also a car." $(\mathbf{B}_i[\Phi] \wedge \mathbf{B}_i[\neg\Phi])$
- "The object is blue." $(\neg\mathbf{B}_i[\Phi] \wedge \neg\mathbf{B}_i[\neg\Phi])$

- "The object is a car." $(\neg \mathbf{B}_i[\Phi] \wedge \mathbf{B}_i[\neg\Phi])$

A.3.2 Insertions

An insertion is of the form

```
(INSERT-DATA-TOKEN token01)
```

where `token01` is an instance of a data token:

```
token01
  :SPATIAL-DESCRIPTION   (V1 V2)
  :SEMANTIC-DESCRIPTION  (LARGE RED POST)
  :HEIGHT                7.3
            . . .
```

Executing (`INSERT-DATA-TOKEN token01`) has the same effect as asserting

$$\mathbf{B}_i[V_1(\text{token01})] \ \wedge \ \mathbf{B}_i[V_2(\text{token01})] \ \wedge$$
$$\mathbf{B}_i[LARGE(\text{token01})] \ \wedge \ \mathbf{B}_i[RED(\text{token01})] \ \wedge \ \mathbf{B}_i[POST(\text{token01})]$$

Assertions about objects can only be in the form of a conjunction of properties. This approach allows an agent to assert that `token02` is a GREEN HOUSE but does not allow him to say, for example, that `token02` is either a HOUSE or a BARN. If an agent desires to convey this information, he must rephrase it as, for example, `token02` is a BUILDING, with the attendant loss of information. If it is truly important for a process to convey this disjunction precisely, the vocabulary should be extended to include HOUSE-OR-BARN as an acceptable term. It is our expectation that processes will need to communicate only in terms similar to those that have evolved for human communication, and as a result, that there will be little need to resort to such artificial constructs as HOUSE-OR-BARN.

A.3.3 Queries

The syntax of the query language is provided in Figure A.1. The language differs from traditional query languages because the CKS database contains information that is both incomplete and inconsistent. The query language must provide the user with a means for discerning multiple opinions. For this reason, the query language qualifiers **APPARENTLY** and **POSSIBLY** are provided to make these distinctions. Loosely speaking, a WFF is true "apparently" if there is some agent that believes it. It is true "possibly" if there is some agent who believes it or there is no agent that believes that it is false. These notions will be formalized shortly.

As can be seen in Figure A.1, queries are either simple or compound. Simple queries are a list of three items: a *qualifier*, a *relation*, and an *argument*. The argument is a semantic or spatial description or something else, depending upon the identity of the relation. Each relation is in reality a three-valued predicate, with "I don't know" being an acceptable value. This allows the user of the CKS to reason appropriately when information is either lacking or inconsistent. Currently four relations are provided:

IN — This relation is interpreted as being satisfied only by those data tokens that are contained within the volume denoted by the argument, which must be a spatial description.

IS — This relation is satisfied by those tokens that belong to the class denoted by the argument, which must be a semantic description.

HAS-AS-PART — This relation is satisfied by those data tokens of which the argument is believed to be a component.

IS-PART-OF — The data tokens that satisfy this relation are those that are believed to be components of its argument.

Additional relations may also be defined for use in retrievals—this facility is described in section A.3.4.

Each relation divides the universe of objects into three sets relative to its argument(s): those that are known to satisfy the relation, those that are known to not satisfy the relation, and those for which no determination is possible. The qualifiers, "apparently" and "possibly" are used to indicate which sets are desired in any particular query. To describe the semantics of qualified queries, there are two cases to consider: those queries for which only a single agent has provided a relevant opinion, and those for which more than one agent is involved.

First, we enumerate the situations in which there is only a single agent. Φ is "apparently" true for the following combinations of beliefs of an agent:

Belief about Φ **APPARENTLY** Belief about $\neg\Phi$	$\mathbf{B}_i[\Phi]$	$\neg\mathbf{B}_i[\Phi]$
$\neg\mathbf{B}_i[\neg\Phi]$	Yes	No
$\mathbf{B}_i[\neg\Phi]$	Yes	No

Similarly, Φ is "possibly" true for the following combinations of belief:

Belief about Φ **POSSIBLY** Belief about $\neg\Phi$	$\mathbf{B}_i[\Phi]$	$\neg\mathbf{B}_i[\Phi]$
$\neg\mathbf{B}_i[\neg\Phi]$	Yes	Yes
$\mathbf{B}_i[\neg\Phi]$	Yes	No

Before providing exact formulas for the interpretation of CKS queries, we examine those situations in which Φ is "apparently" and "possibly" true when there are two agents involved.

Φ is "apparently" true for the following combinations of beliefs of two agents:

Beliefs of Agent 2 **APPARENTLY** Beliefs of Agent 1	$\mathbf{B}_2[\Phi]$ $\wedge$ $\neg\mathbf{B}_2[\neg\Phi]$	$\mathbf{B}_2[\Phi]$ $\wedge$ $\mathbf{B}_2[\neg\Phi]$	$\neg\mathbf{B}_2[\Phi]$ $\wedge$ $\neg\mathbf{B}_2[\neg\Phi]$	$\neg\mathbf{B}_2[\Phi]$ $\wedge$ $\mathbf{B}_2[\neg\Phi]$
$\mathbf{B}_1[\Phi] \wedge \neg\mathbf{B}_1[\neg\Phi]$	Yes	Yes	Yes	Yes
$\mathbf{B}_1[\Phi] \wedge \mathbf{B}_1[\neg\Phi]$	Yes	Yes	Yes	Yes
$\neg\mathbf{B}_1[\Phi] \wedge \neg\mathbf{B}_1[\neg\Phi]$	Yes	Yes	No	No
$\neg\mathbf{B}_1[\Phi] \wedge \mathbf{B}_1[\neg\Phi]$	Yes	Yes	No	No

Similarly, Φ is "possibly" true for the following combinations of belief:

Beliefs of Agent 2 **POSSIBLY** Beliefs of Agent 1	$\mathbf{B}_2[\Phi]$ $\wedge$ $\neg\mathbf{B}_2[\neg\Phi]$	$\mathbf{B}_2[\Phi]$ $\wedge$ $\mathbf{B}_2[\neg\Phi]$	$\neg\mathbf{B}_2[\Phi]$ $\wedge$ $\neg\mathbf{B}_2[\neg\Phi]$	$\neg\mathbf{B}_2[\Phi]$ $\wedge$ $\mathbf{B}_2[\neg\Phi]$
$\mathbf{B}_1[\Phi] \wedge \neg\mathbf{B}_1[\neg\Phi]$	Yes	Yes	Yes	Yes
$\mathbf{B}_1[\Phi] \wedge \mathbf{B}_1[\neg\Phi]$	Yes	Yes	Yes	Yes
$\neg\mathbf{B}_1[\Phi] \wedge \neg\mathbf{B}_1[\neg\Phi]$	Yes	Yes	Yes	No
$\neg\mathbf{B}_1[\Phi] \wedge \mathbf{B}_1[\neg\Phi]$	Yes	Yes	No	No

By extrapolating these results, we are in a position to describe the interpretation of each query in terms of our modal logic.

- (FIND-IDS (APPARENTLY IS W4)) returns a list of those objects in the set

$$\{x \mid (\exists i)\mathbf{B}_i[W_4(x)]\}$$

where W4 denotes a vocabulary word. In English, this query corresponds roughly to "Find each data token for which some agent believes W_4 is true of it."

- (FIND-IDS (POSSIBLY IS W4)) returns a list of those objects in the set

$$\{x \mid [(\exists i)\mathbf{B}_i[W_4(x)] \vee \neg(\exists i)\mathbf{B}_i[\neg W_4(x)]]\}$$

This query can be roughly translated as "Find each data token for which some agent believes W_4 could possibly be true." The set of objects which satisfy this query will always include those objects that satisfy the APPARENTLY version.

- (FIND-IDS (APPARENTLY IN V3)) returns a list of those objects in the set

$$\{x \mid (\exists i)\mathbf{B}_i[V_3(x)]\}$$

where V3 is a spatial description. This query can be interpreted as "Find each data token such that some agent believes it is contained within the volume V_3."

- (FIND-IDS (POSSIBLY IN V3)) returns a list of those objects in the set

$$\{x \mid [(\exists i)\mathbf{B}_i[V_3(x)] \vee \neg(\exists i)\mathbf{B}_i[\neg V_3(x)]]\}$$

This query can be interpreted to mean "Find each data token such that some agent believes that it could possibly be in the volume denoted by V_3."

- (FIND-IDS (AND Query1 Query2))

    $\{x \mid x \in$ (FIND-IDS Query1) $\wedge x \in$ (FIND-IDS Query2)$\}$.

    In English, this can be translated as "Find each data token that satisfies both Query1 and Query2. It can be thought of as the intersection of the sets of tokens that satisfy each query.

- (FIND-IDS (OR Query1 Query2))

    $\{x \mid x \in$ (FIND-IDS Query1) $\vee x \in$ (FIND-IDS Query2)$\}$.

    This can be translated as "Find each data token that satisfies either Query1 or Query2. It can be thought of as the union of the sets of tokens that satisfy each query.

- (FIND-IDS (AND-NOT Query1 Query2))

    $\{x \mid x \in$ (FIND-IDS Query1) $\wedge x \notin$ (FIND-IDS Query2)$\}$.

    This query can be interpreted to mean "Find all data tokens that satisfy Query1 but that do not also satisfy Query2. In set-theoretic terms, it is the set difference of the sets of data tokens that satisfy Query1 and Query2.

In answering negative queries, the database has no Closed World Assumption (i.e., it does not assume that a proposition is false if it cannot be proved true), thus it avoids issues of nonmonotonicity and has no need for circumscription. A negative belief cannot be inserted in the database. However, a negative belief can be deduced using the deductive inference axiom and the general knowledge incorporated in the vocabulary. For example, a process cannot assert that token03 is not a PINE. But if it does assert that the token is an OAK, (i.e., $\mathbf{B}_i[OAK(\text{token03})]$), the database will infer that $\mathbf{B}_i[\neg PINE(\text{token03})]$.

A.3.4   USER–DEFINED RELATIONS

In addition to the predefined relations, a new relation can be defined by providing a LISP function as the relation in a query. It may take any arguments that are appropriate for it, but must return T, NIL or :MAYBE. For example, a relation WEIGHS-MORE-THAN could be defined as follows:

```
(defun WEIGHS-MORE-THAN (token ref-weight)
  (let ((weight
           (RETRIEVE-SLOT-OPINION token :WEIGHT 'LATEST)))
     (cond ((null weight) :MAYBE)
           ((> weight ref-weight) T)
           (T NIL))))
```

Programmers who write procedural relations are cautioned to write them efficiently. While the transaction parser will attempt to optimize the query evaluation, nevertheless it will sometimes be forced to evaluate the relation on a large list of data tokens.

The qualifier is used to interpret the results of the three-valued predicate's evaluation of each data token in order to construct the list of tokens that are to be returned:

APPARENTLY — The list returned contains only those tokens for which the function evaluates to T.

POSSIBLY — The list includes all those tokens for which the function evaluates to T or :MAYBE.

For the standard relations, the above description indicates the effect of a query, but not the implementation. The actual algorithm used for the standard relations is much different in order to achieve high performance on very large databases.

A.3.5 DISCUSSION

There are several restrictions upon the statements that an agent can make about the world and on the types of queries that can be posed. These restrictions were necessary to enable a practical implementation of the database.

The query language only allows a limited variety of queries. Acceptable queries are limited both by their syntax and by the vocabulary of properties. The query language is not intended to be a universal language. We have designed it so that the only queries that can be posed are those that can usually be retrieved efficiently, given our database architecture. It is important to bear in mind that the limitation of the query language is one that restricts only what questions can be answered efficiently; it does not prevent the identification of data tokens that satisfy an unusual query. When faced with a question that cannot be posed as a syntactically legal query, a user can obtain the exact retrieval by first retrieving a superset of the desired data tokens with an acceptable query, and then examining each token in that set individually for satisfaction of the intended query.

A.4 Slot Access

The query language described in the previous section provides the means to insert data tokens into the CKS database and to retrieve pointers to those tokens based upon spatial and semantic criteria. In this section, the various mechanisms for gaining access to the information contained within a data token are described.

Data tokens are stored as frames consisting of a number of slots. Externally, each slot has a single value. Internally, however, a separate value is maintained for each process that offers an opinion. Conceptually, an association list that pairs the process name with its opinion is stored for each slot:

SLOT-NAME: ((P1 . V1) (P2 . V2) ...)

When retrieving a slot's value, one specifies the combination method desired to combine all values that have been previously provided for that slot. This approach makes it possible to integrate multiple opinions in a manner that is suited to the task at hand. For example, if a robot wants to determine whether its camera will have an unobstructed view over a fence, it should use that opinion that has the greatest value for the HEIGHT slot. On the other hand, if its goal is to keep all the cows in a confined area, it should be interested in the smallest value of HEIGHT.

The following function is used to store a new opinion as the value of a slot:

(INSERT-SLOT-OPINION <id> <slot> <value>
                     &optional <auxiliary-data-fields>)

INSERT-SLOT-OPINION causes <value> to be stored as the opinion of the calling process for the <slot> of the data token denoted by <id>.

If the process has already provided an opinion, it is replaced by <value>. The strength of belief and time of belief may be specified in <auxiliary-data-fields>. If present, this information is stored in the internal representation and can be retrieved with RETRIEVE-SLOT-OPINION. If <slot> is not the name of a currently known slot in <id>, a new slot is created—this provides the facility for a user to extend a data token so as to include a slot of his own choosing.

Slot values are retrieved from data tokens using the function:

(RETRIEVE-SLOT-OPINION <id> <slot> <arbitrator>)

RETRIEVE-SLOT-OPINION returns two values. The first can be viewed as the value of <slot> for data token <id>. The particular value returned is determined by <arbitrator>, which specifies how multiple opinions are to be integrated by this invocation of RETRIEVE-SLOT-OPINION. The second value contains the auxiliary data associated with the returned opinion. The <arbitrator> can be any from the following list, or a programmer can use a special-purpose procedure by supplying it as the value of <arbitrator>. Additional arbitrators may be added in the future to support a larger variety of techniques for information integration.

The functionality of each choice is as follows:

DEFAULT returns the default value stored in the semantic network, and possibly inherited from a superclass. This default can be considered as another opinion of the value of the slot on the object denoted by <id>.

LATEST returns the opinion that was most recently provided to the CKS.

MIN returns the smallest of all the opinions. MIN uses arithmetic comparison if its arguments are numeric, uses alphabetic comparison for arguments that are strings or symbols, and is undefined otherwise.

MAX returns the largest of all the opinions.

AVG returns the arithmetic average of all the opinions. It ignores any opinion that is nonnumeric.

(PROCESS <proc-name>) returns the opinion that was most recently provided by the process denoted by <proc-name>.

LIST returns a list of all opinions that have been rendered.

ALIST returns an alist of all the opinions. Each pair is of the form (`<proc-name>` . `<value>`), where `<proc-name>` is the name of a process, and `<value>` is the most recent opinion provided by that process.

`<procedure>` is the name of a function or a lambda expression provided by the programmer. Its single argument is the result that would have been returned if ALIST had been used. `<procedure>` should return a value that is to be viewed as the integration of all opinions. For example, a simple implementation of an opinion preference scheme could be implemented by: (RETRIEVE-SLOT-OPINION `<id>` 'PRIORITY `<slot>`), where PRIORITY is defined as

```
(defun PRIORITY (alist)
    (or (cdr (assq Process-1 alist))
        (cdr (assq Process-2 alist))
        (cdar alist)))
```

It is also possible to retrieve an entire data token, given a token `<id>`.

(RETRIEVE-DATA-TOKEN `<id>` &optional `<slot-process-alist>`)

Given a data token `<id>`, this function returns a flavor instance whose slots are filled with values as determined by the optional argument. By default, each slot receives the most recent opinion expressed by any process (i.e., LATEST). To override the default, a pair of the form (`<slot>` `<arbitrator>`) is included on the `<slot-process-alist>`.

A.5 Summary

We have described an information storage and retrieval mechanism that avoids the requirement of consistency maintenance imposed by traditional knowledge-based systems. By viewing data as opinions rather than facts, the system is able to combine knowledge that is generally accepted as being true with data that may be from unreliable sources. We have also given a formal account of the semantics of such an approach.

The design differs significantly from other data management systems by allowing information to be integrated at retrieval time rather than requiring all data to be made consistent at insertion time. While this requires storage of a larger volume of data than would be required by other data management systems, it has several significant advantages:

- It affords the opportunity to integrate information according to the demands of the current task.

- It allows the use of information that may not be available at insertion time.

- It eliminates the need for fusing information that is irrelevant to the ongoing task.

The information management system described has been implemented and incorporated within the Core Knowledge Structure. It has been used to store information derived from image processing along with opinions from other sources and from users. It appears to be well-suited for the requirements of an autonomous robot, and for information storage in general.

```
<transaction> ::= (FIND-IDS <query>)  |
                  (FIND-CLASSES <query>)  |
                  (INSERT-DATA-TOKEN <data-token>)  |
                  (RETRIEVE-DATA-TOKEN <id> <slot-process-alist>) |
                  (INSERT-SLOT-OPINION <id> <slot> <value>)  |
                  (RETRIEVE-SLOT-OPINION <id> <slot> <arbitrator>)


<query>  ::=  <simple-query>  |  <compound-query>


<simple-query> ::= (<qualifier> IN <spatial-description>) |
                   (<qualifier> IS <semantic-description>) |
                   (<qualifier> HAS-AS-PART <semantic-description>)|
                   (<qualifier> IS-PART-OF <semantic-description>) |
                   (<qualifier> <3-valued-relation> [<args> ...] )


<compound-query> ::=    (OR <query> ... <query>)  |
                        (AND <query> ... <query>)  |
                        (AND-NOT <query> <query>)



<qualifier> ::=  APPARENTLY  |  POSSIBLY



<semantic-description> ::= (<vocabulary-word> ... <vocabulary-word>)




<arbitrator>  ::= DEFAULT  |  LATEST  |  MIN  |  MAX  |  AVG  |
                  (PROCESS <process-name>)  |
                  LIST  |  ALIST  |
                  <procedure>
```

FIGURE A.1. Syntax for the CKS Query Language.

REFERENCES

[Agin 1972] Agin, G.J., "Representation and Description of Curved Objects," Ph.D. Dissertation, AIM-173, AI Laboratory, Stanford University, Stanford, CA (October 1972).

[Agin and Binford 1973] Agin, G.J., and T.O. Binford, "Computer Description of Curved Objects," *Proceedings 3rd International Joint Conference on Artificial Intelligence*, pp. 629–640 (1973).

[Baker and Bolles 1988] Baker, Harlyn H., and Robert C. Bolles, "Generalizing Epipolar-Plane Image Analysis on the Spatiotemporal Surface," *Proceedings: DARPA Image Understanding Workshop*, Cambridge, MA, pp. 1022–1030 (April 1988).

[Ballard, Brown, and Feldman 1978] Ballard, D.H., C.M. Brown, and J.A. Feldman, "An Approach to Knowledge-Directed Image Analysis," *Proceedings 5th International Joint Conference on Artificial Intelligence*, Cambridge, MA, pp. 664–670 (August 1977).

[Ballard and Brown 1982] Ballard, Dana H., and Christopher M. Brown, *Computer Vision*, Prentice-Hall, Inc., Englewood Cliffs, NJ (1982).

[Barnard and Fischler 1982] Barnard, Stephen T., and Martin A. Fischler, "Computational Stereo," *Computing Surveys*, Vol. 14, No. 4, pp. 553–572 (December 1982).

[Barnard 1989] Barnard, Stephen T., "Stochastic Stereo Matching over Scale," *International Journal of Computer Vision*, Vol. 3, No. 1, pp. 17 – 32 (1989).

[Barrow and Tenenbaum 1976] Barrow, Harry G., and Jay M. Tenenbaum, "MSYS: A System for Reasoning about Scenes," Technical Note 121, Artificial Intelligence Center, SRI International, Menlo Park, CA (April 1976).

[Barrow *et. al.* 1977] Barrow, Harry G., Thomas D. Garvey, Jan Kremers, J. Martin Tenenbaum, and Helen C. Wolf, "Interactive Aids for Cartography and Interpretation," Technical Note 137, Artificial Intelligence Center, SRI International, Menlo Park, CA (January 1977).

[Barrow and Tenenbaum 1977] Barrow, Harry G., and Jay M. Tenenbaum, "Experiments in Model-Driven Scene Segmentation," *Artificial Intelligence*, Vol. 8, No. 3, pp. 241–274 (June 1977).

[Biederman 1988] Biederman, Irving, "Aspects and Extensions of a Theory of Human Image Understanding," Chapter 14 in Zenon Pylyshyn (Ed.), *Computational Processes in Human Vision: An Interdisciplinary Perspective*, Ablex Publishing Corporation, Norwood, NJ (1988).

[Binford 1982] Binford, T.O., "Survey of Model-Based Image Analysis Systems," *Int. J. Robotics Research*, Vol. 1, pp. 18–64 (1982).

[Bolles, Horaud, and Hannah 1983] Bolles, R.C., R. Horaud, and M.J. Hannah, "3DPO: A 3D Part Orientation System," in *Proceedings 8th International Joint Conference on Artificial Intelligence*, Karlsruhe, West Germany, pp. 1116–1120 (August 1983).

[Brooks 1983] Brooks, Rodney A., "Model-Based 3-D Interpretations of 2-D Images," *IEEE Transactions on Pattern Analysis and Machine Intelligence*, Vol. 5, No. 2, pp. 140–150 (March 1983).

[Cavanagh 1987] Cavanagh, P., "Reconstructing the third dimension: Interaction between color, texture, motion, binocular disparity, and shape," in *Computer Vision, Graphics and Image Processing* (1987).

[Draper et. al. 1989] Draper, Bruce A., Robert T. Collins, John Brolio, Allen R. Hanson, and Edward M. Riseman, "The Schema System," *International Journal of Computer Vision*, Vol. 2, No. 3, pp. 209–250 (January 1989). 192z

[Faugeras and Hebert 1983] Faugeras, O.D., and M. Hebert, "A 3-D Recognition and Positioning Algorithm using Geometrical Matching Between Primitive Surfaces," *Proceedings 8th International Joint Conference on Artificial Intelligence*, Karlsruhe, West Germany, pp. 996–1002 (August 1983).

[Feldman and Yakimovsky 1974] Feldman, Jerome A., and Yoram Yakimovsky, "Decision Theory and AI: A Semantics-Based Region Analyzer," *Artificial Intelligence*, Vol. 5, No. 4, pp. 349–371 (1974).

[Fischler and Elschlager 1973] Fischler, Martin A., and R. A. Elschlager, "The Representation and Matching of Pictorial Structures," *IEEE Transactions on Computers*, Vol. C-22, No. 1, pp. 67–92 (January 1973).

[Fischler, Bolles, and Smith 1982] Fischler, Martin A., Robert C. Bolles, and Grahame Smith, "Modeling and Using Physical Constraints in Scene Analysis," Technical Note 267, Artificial Intelligence Center, SRI International, Menlo Park, CA (September 1982).

[Fischler and Wolf 1983] Fischler, Martin A., and Helen C. Wolf, "Linear Delineation," Proceedings IEEE Conference on Computer Vision and Pattern Recognition, Washington, DC, pp. 351–356 (June 1983).

[Fischler and Bolles 1986] Fischler, Martin A., and Bolles, R.C., "Perceptual Organization and Curve Partitioning," *IEEE Transactions on Pattern Analysis and Machine Intelligence*, Volume 8, Number 1, pp. 100–105 (January 1986).

[Fischler and Firschein 1987a] Fischler, Martin A., and Oscar Firschein, *Intelligence: The Eye, the Brain, and the Computer,* Addison-Wesley Publishing Co., Reading, MA (1987).

[Fischler and Firschein 1987b] Fischler, Martin A., and Oscar Firschein, *Readings in Computer Vision,* Morgan Kaufmann Publishers, Inc., Los Altos, CA (1987).

[Fischler and Strat 1988] Fischler, Martin A., and Thomas M. Strat, "Recognizing Trees, Bushes, Rocks and Rivers," *Proceedings of the AAAI Spring Symposium Series: Physical and Biological Approaches to Computational Vision,* Stanford University, Stanford, CA, pp. 62–64 (March 1988).

[Fischler and Strat 1989] Fischler, Martin A., and Thomas M. Strat, "Recognizing Objects in a Natural Environment: A Contextual Vision System," *Proceedings: DARPA Image Understanding Workshop,* Palo Alto, CA, pp. 774–796 (May 1989).

[Fua and Hanson 1987] Fua, Pascal, and Andrew J. Hanson, "Using Generic Geometric Models for Intelligent Shape Extraction," *Proceedings: DARPA Image Understanding Workshop,* Los Angeles, CA, pp. 227–233 (February 1987).

[Garvey 1975] Garvey, Thomas D., "Perceptual Strategies for Purposive Vision," Ph.D. Dissertation, Department of Electrical Engineering, Stanford University, Stanford, CA (December 1975).

[Genesereth and Nilsson 1987] Genesereth, Michael R., and Nils J. Nilsson, *Logical Foundations of Artificial Intelligence,* Morgan Kaufmann Publishers, Inc., Los Altos, CA (1987).

[Goad 1983] Goad, C., "Special Purpose Automatic Programming for 3D Model-Based Vision," in *Proceedings: DARPA Image Understanding Workshop*, Arlington, VA, pp. 94–104 (June 1983).

[Grimson and Lozano-Perez 1984] Grimson, W.E.L., and T. Lozano-Perez, "Model-Based Recognition from Sparse Range or Tactile Data," *International Journal of Robotics Research*, Vol. 3, No. 3, pp. 3–35 (1984).

[Hannah 1985] Hannah, M.J., "SRI's Baseline Stereo System," *Proceedings: DARPA Image Understanding Workshop*, Miami Beach, FL, pp. 149–155 (December 1985).

[Hanson and Riseman 1978] Hanson, A.R., and E.M. Riseman, "VISIONS: A Computer System for Interpreting Scenes," in *Computer Vision Systems*, Academic Press, New York, pp. 303–333 (1978).

[Hanson and Quam 1988] Hanson, Andrew J., and Lynn Quam, "Overview of the SRI Cartographic Modeling Environment," *Proceedings: DARPA Image Understanding Workshop*, Cambridge, MA, pp. 576–582 (April 1988).

[Herman and Kanade 1984] Herman, M., and T. Kanade, "The 3D MOSAIC Scene Understanding System: Incremental Reconstruction of 3D Scenes from Complex Images," in *Proceedings: DARPA Image Understanding Workshop*, New Orleans, LA, pp. 137–148 (October 1984).

[Hoffman and Richards 1985] Hoffman, D.D., and W.A. Richards, "Parts of Recognition," *Cognition*, Vol. 18, pp. 65–96 (1985).

[Horn 1989] Horn, Berthold K.P., "Height and Gradient from Shading," MIT AI Memo No. 1105, Artificial Intelligence Laboratory, Massachusetts Institute of Technology, Cambridge, MA (May 1989).

[Huttenlocher and Ullman 1988] Huttenlocher, Daniel P., and Shimon Ullman, "Recognizing Solid Objects by Alignment," *Proceedings: DARPA Image Understanding Workshop*, Cambridge, MA, pp. 1114–1122 (April 1988).

[Hwang 1984] Hwang, S. V., "Evidence Accumulation for Spatial Reasoning in Aerial Image Understanding," Ph.D. Dissertation, University of Maryland, College Park, MD (1984).

[Jain 1989] Jain, Ramesh, "Building an Environment Model Using Depth Information," Working Paper, Artificial Intelligence Laboratory, University of Michigan, Ann Arbor, MI (1989).

[Kass, Witkin, and Terzopoulos 1987] Kass, Michael, Andrew Witkin, and Demitri Terzopoulos, "Snakes: Active Contour Models," *Proceedings, ICCV,* London, England, pp. 259–268 (June 1987).

[Konolige 1984] Konolige, Kurt, "A Deduction Model of Belief and its Logic," SRI Artificial Intelligence Center Technical Note 326, SRI International, Menlo Park, CA (August 1984).

[Kriegman and Binford 1988] Kriegman, David J., and Thomas O. Binford, "Generic Models for Robot Navigation," *Proceedings: DARPA Image Understanding Workshop,* Cambridge, MA, pp. 453–460 (April 1988).

[Laws 1988] Laws, Kenneth, I., "Integrated Split/Merge Image Segmentation," Technical Note 441, Artificial Intelligence Center, SRI International, Menlo Park, CA (July 1988).

[Marr and Nishihara 1978] Marr, David, and H. Keith Nishihara, "Visual Information Processing: Artificial Intelligence and the Sensorium of Sight," *Technology Review,* Vol. 81, No. 1, pp. 2–23 (October 1978).

[Marr 1982] Marr, David, *Vision,* W.H. Freeman, San Francisco, CA (1982).

[McKeown, Harvey, and McDermott 1985] McKeown, David M., Jr., W.A. Harvey, Jr., and J. McDermott, "Rule-Based Interpretation of Aerial Imagery," *IEEE Transactions on Pattern Analysis and Machine Intelligence,* Vol. 7, No. 5, pp. 570–585 (September 1985).

[McKeown and Denlinger 1988] McKeown, David M., Jr., and Jerry L. Denlinger, "Cooperative Methods for Road Tracking in Aerial Imagery," *Proceedings: DARPA Image Understanding Workshop,* Cambridge, MA, pp. 327–341 (April 1988).

[Mitchell 1978] Mitchell, Thomas M., "Version Spaces: An Approach to Concept Learning," Ph.D. Dissertation, Computer Science Department, Stanford University, Stanford, CA (December 1978).

[Moore and Hendrix 1979] Moore, Robert C., and Gary G. Hendrix, "Computational Models of Belief and the Semantics of Belief Sentences," SRI Artificial Intelligence Center Technical Note 187, SRI International, Menlo Park, CA (1979).

[Nagao and Matsuyama 1980] Nagao, M. and T. Matsuyama, *A Structural Analysis of Complex Aerial Photographs,* Sherman Press, Plenum, New York (1980).

[Nevatia 1974] Nevatia, Ramankant, "Structured Descriptions of Complex Curved Objects for Recognition and Visual Memory," AIM-250, AI Laboratory, Stanford University, Stanford, CA (October 1974).

[Ohta 1980] Ohta, Yuichi, "A Region-Oriented Image-Analysis System by Computer," Doctoral dissertation, Information Science Department, Kyoto University, Kyoto, Japan (1980).

[Pentland 1986a] Pentland, Alexander P., "Perceptual Organization and Representation of Natural Form," *J. Artificial Intelligence,* Vol. 28, pp. 293–331 (1986).

[Pentland 1986b] Pentland, Alexander, (Ed.), *From Pixels to Predicates,* Ablex, Norwood, NJ (1986).

[Ponce and Kriegman 1989] Ponce, Jean, and David J. Kriegman, "On Recognizing and Positioning Curved 3D Objects from Image Contours," *Proceedings: DARPA Image Understanding Workshop,* Palo Alto, CA, pp. 461–470 (May 1989).

[Roberts 1965] Roberts, L. G., "Machine Perception of Three-Dimensional Solids," in *Optical and Electro-optical Information Processing,* J.P. Tippett (Ed.), MIT Press, Cambridge, MA (1965).

[Rosenfeld, Hummel, and Zucker 1976] Rosenfeld, A., R.A. Hummel, and S.W. Zucker, "Scene Labeling by Relaxation Operations," *IEEE Transactions on Systems, Man, and Cybernetics,* Vol. 6, No. 6, pp. 420–433 (June 1976).

[Shirai and Suwa 1971] Shirai, Y., and M. Suwa, "Recognition of Polyhedrons with a Rangefinder," *Proceedings of the Second International Joint Conference on Artificial Intelligence,* London, England, pp. 80–87 (1971).

[Sloan 1977] Sloan, Kenneth R., Jr., "World Model Driven Recognition of Natural Scenes," PhD Thesis, Moore School of Electrical Engineering, University of Pennsylvania, Philadelphia, PA (June 1977).

[Smith and Strat 1986] Smith, Grahame B., and Thomas M. Strat, "A Knowledge-Based Architecture for Organizing Sensory Data," *International Autonomous Systems Congress Proceedings,* Amsterdam, Netherlands (December 1986).

[Smith and Strat 1987] Smith, Grahame B., and Thomas M. Strat, "Information Management in a Sensor-Based Autonomous System," *Proceedings:*

DARPA Image Understanding Workshop, Los Angeles, CA, pp. 170–177 (February 1987).

[Strat 1979] Strat, Thomas M., "A Numerical Method for Shape-from-Shading from a Single Image," S.M. Thesis, Department of Electrical Engineering and Computer Science, Massachusetts Institute of Technology, Cambridge, MA (January 1979).

[Strat 1984a] Strat, Thomas M., "Spatial Reasoning from Line Drawings of Polyhedra," *Proceedings IEEE Workshop on Computer Vision: Representation and Control,* Annapolis, MD, pp. 219–224 (April 1984).

[Strat 1984b] Strat, Thomas M., "Recovering the Camera Parameters from a Transformation Matrix," *Proceedings DARPA Image Understanding Workshop,* New Orleans, LA, pp. 230–235 (October 1984).

[Strat and Fischler 1986] Strat, Thomas M. and Martin A. Fischler, "One-Eyed Stereo: A General Approach to Modeling 3-D Scene Geometry," in *IEEE Transactions on Pattern Analysis and Machine Intelligence,* Vol. 8, No. 6, pp. 730–741 (November 1986).

[Strat and Smith 1987a] Strat, Thomas M., and Grahame B. Smith, "The Core Knowledge System," Technical Note 426, Artificial Intelligence Center, SRI International, Menlo Park, CA, (October 1987).

[Strat and Smith 1987b] Strat, Thomas M., and Grahame B. Smith, "The Management of Spatial Information in a Mobile Robot," *Proceedings of the Workshop on Spatial Reasoning and Multi-Sensor Fusion,* Chicago, IL, pp. 240 – 249 (October 1987).

[Strat and Smith 1988a] Strat, Thomas M. and Grahame B. Smith, "Core Knowledge System: Storage and Retrieval of Inconsistent Information," *Proceedings, DARPA Image Understanding Workshop,* Cambridge, MA, pp. 660–665 (April 1988).

[Strat and Smith 1988b] Strat, Thomas M. and Grahame B. Smith, "A Knowledge-Based Information Manager for Autonomous Vehicles," Chapter 1 in Su-shing Chen (Ed.), *Image Understanding in Unstructured Environments*, World Scientific Publishing Co., Singapore, pp. 1–39 (1988).

[Strat and Fischler 1989] Strat, Thomas M. and Martin A. Fischler, "Context-Based Vision: Recognition of Natural Scenes," *Proceedings of the 23rd Asilomar Conference on Signals, Systems, and Man,* Pacific Grove, CA, pp. 532–536 (October 1989).

[Strat and Fischler 1990] Strat, Thomas M. and Martin A. Fischler, "A Context-Based Recognition System for Natural Scenes and Complex Domains," *Proceedings, DARPA Image Understanding Workshop*, Pittsburgh, PA, pp. 456–472 (September 1990).

[Strat 1990] Strat, Thomas M., "Natural Object Recognition," Ph. D. Dissertation, Report No. STAN-CS-91-1376, Computer Science Department, Stanford University, Stanford, CA (December 1990).

[Swain 1990] Swain, Michael, "Color Indexing," Ph.D. Thesis, Computer Science Department, University of Rochester, Rochester, NY (1990).

[Tenenbaum 1973] Tenenbaum, Jay M., "On Locating Objects by Their Distinguishing Features in Multisensory Images," *Computer Graphics and Image Processing*, pp. 308–320 (December 1973).

[Tenenbaum and Weyl 1975] Tenenbaum, Jay M. and S. Weyl, "A Region Analysis Subsystem for Interactive Scene Analysis," *Proceedings of the Fourth International Joint Conference on Artificial Intelligence*, Tbilisi, Georgia, USSR, pp. 682–687 (September 1975).

[Tenenbaum and Barrow 1976] Tenenbaum, Jay M., and Harry G. Barrow, "Experiments in Interpretation-Guided Segmentation," Technical Note 123, Artificial Intelligence Center, SRI International, Menlo Park, CA (March 1976).

[Tenenbaum, Fischler, and Wolf 1978] Tenenbaum, Jay M., Martin A. Fischler, and Helen C. Wolf, "A Scene Analysis Approach to Remote Sensing," Technical Note 173, Artificial Intelligence Center, SRI International, Menlo Park, CA (October 1978).

[Tenenbaum et. al. 1979] Tenenbaum, Jay M., Harry G. Barrow, Robert C. Bolles, Martin A. Fischler, and Helen C. Wolf, "Map-Guided Interpretation of Remotely-Sensed Imagery," *Pattern Recognition and Image Processing*, pp. 610–617 (February 1979).

[Tenenbaum, Fischler, and Barrow 1980] Tenenbaum, Jay M., Martin A. Fischler, and Harry G. Barrow, "A Scene Analysis Approach to Remote Sensing," Technical Note 221, Artificial Intelligence Center, SRI International, Menlo Park, CA (July 1980).

[Terzopoulos, Witkin, and Kass 1987] Terzopoulos, Demitri, Andrew Witkin, and Michael Kass, "Symmetry-seeking models for 3D object reconstruction," *International Journal of Computer Vision*, Vol. 1, No. 3, pp. 211–221 (1987).

[Treisman 1985] Treisman, A., "Preattentive Processing in Vision," *Computer Vision, Graphics, and Image Processing*, Vol. 31, No. 2, pp. 156–177 (August 1985).

[Tsotsos 1988] Tsotsos, John K., "A Complexity Level Analysis of Immediate Vision," *International Journal of Computer Vision*, Vol. 1, No. 4, pp. 303–320 (1988).

[Tsuji and Nakao 1981] Tsuji, Saburo, and Hidetoshi Nakano, "Knowledge-Based Identification of Artery Branches in Cine-Angiograms," *Proceedings 7th International Joint Conference on Artificial Intelligence*, Vancouver, B.C., Canada, pp. 710–715 (August 1981).

[Waltz 1972] Waltz, D.I., "Generating Semantic Descriptions from Drawings of Scenes With Shadows," Ph.D. Dissertation, Artificial Intelligence Laboratory, Massachusetts Institute of Technology, Cambridge, MA (1972).

[Yakimovsky and Feldman 1973] Yakimovksy, Yoram, and Jerome A. Feldman, "A Semantics-Based Decision Theory Region Analyzer," *Proceedings of the Third Joint Conference on Artificial Intelligence*, Stanford, CA, pp. 580–588 (August 1973).